Business titles from Adams Media Corporation

Accounting for the New Business, by Christopher R. Malburg
Adams Businesses You Can Start Almanac, by Katina Jones
Adams Streetwise Complete Business Plan, by Bob Adams
Adams Streetwise Consulting, by David Kintler
Adams Streetwise Customer-Focused Selling, by Nancy Stephens
Adams Streetwise Do-It-Yourself Advertising, by Sarah White and John Woods
Adams Streetwise Hiring Top Performers, by Bob Adams and Peter Veruki
Adams Streetwise Managing People, by Bob Adams, et al.
Adams Streetwise Small Business Start-Up, by Bob Adams
All-in-One Business Planner, by Christopher R. Malburg
Buying Your Own Business, by Russell Robb
Entrepreneurial Growth Strategies, by Lawrence W. Tuller
Exporting, Importing, and Beyond, by Lawrence W. Tuller
How to Become Successfully Self-Employed, by Brian R. Smith
How to Start and Operate a Successful Home Business, by David E. Rye
Independent Consultant's Q&A Book, by Lawrence W. Tuller
Management Basics, by John & Shirley Payne
Managing People, by Darien McWhirter
Marketing Magic, by Don Debelak
New A-Z of Managing People, by David Freemantle
The Personnel Policy Handbook for Growing Companies, by Darien McWhirter
Presentations, by Daria Price Bowman
Selling 101: A Course for Business Owners and Non-Sales People,
by Michael T. McGaulley
Service, Service, Service: A Secret Weapon for Your Growing Business,
by Steve Albrecht
The Small Business Legal Kit, by J. W. Dicks
The Small Business Valuation Book, by Lawrence W. Tuller
Streetwise Business Forms, by Bob Adams
Streetwise Business Letters, by John Woods
Streetwise Motivating and Rewarding Employees, by Alexander Hiam
Streetwise Time Management, by Marshall J. Cook

Available through your favorite bookseller.

ADAMS

PUBLIC SPEAKING

Proven Techniques for Giving Successful Talks Every Time

STEVEN FRANK

Adams Media Corporation
Holbrook, Massachusetts

Published by
Adams Media Corporation
260 Center Street, Holbrook, MA 02343 U.S.A.
www.adamsmedia.com

ISBN: 1-58062-184-8

Printed in the United States of America.

J I H G F E D C B

Library of Congress Cataloging-in-Publication Data
Frank, Steven.
Public speaking : proven techniques for giving successful talks
every time / Steven Frank—1st ed.
p.   cm.
ISBN 1-58062-184-8
1. Public speaking. I. Title.
PN4121.F67   1999
808.5'1 21—dc21   99-046083
CIP

This publication is designed to provide accurate and authoritative information with regard
to the subject matter covered. It is sold with the understanding that the publisher is not
engaged in rendering legal, accounting, or other professional advice. If legal advice or
other expert assistance is required, the services of a competent professional person should
be sought.
— From a *Declaration of Principles* jointly adopted by a Committee of the
American Bar Association and a Committee of Publishers and Associations

This book is available at quantity discounts for bulk purchases.
For information, call 1-800-872-5627.

Visit our exciting small business Web site at www.buinesstown.com

CONTENTS

Part II: Delivering Your Speech

Introduction:
What is a Successful Speech?

*Great orators who are not also great writers
become very indistinct shadows to the
generations following them. The spell vanishes
with the voice.*

—THOMAS BAILEY ALDRICH,
LEAVES FROM A NOTEBOOK

From bosses at company meetings to politicians in televised debates, from teachers in the classroom to best men and maids of honor at weddings, we hear examples of public speaking all the time. Most of us, though, don't really consider everything that goes into preparing and delivering a speech, especially what it takes to do so successfully. We don't give it much thought, that is, until someone asks *us* to do it. And make no mistake about it, it will happen to you sooner or later, if it hasn't already. Like death and taxes, it's inevitable that at some point in your life you'll be asked to speak for some personal or professional occasion.

When you start thinking about it more, though, it's not easy to pinpoint what makes a successful speech. Some people believe it's all a matter of the personality of the speaker and the overall impression he or she makes on the listeners. A speaker with "presence," who speaks clearly, confidently, and convincingly with "good timing" is considered to have been effective. Speakers who particularly seem comfortable, making speeches that appear to be effortless and unrehearsed yet polished, are even thought of as "gifted" speakers or "naturals."

But many others argue that it takes more for a speech to be effective than the presence of a charismatic person. What matters is not so much the *way* someone delivers a speech as *what* he or she says. A successful speech is thus dependent on the writing and how much the words communicate, teach, move, and inspire those who hear them.

The reality, of course, is somewhere in between. The speaker's personality and charisma do count for a great deal and are qualities that do make a lasting impression on the audience. In time, people might only remember a small portion of what you said during your speech, but the impression they get of the kind of person you are will be far more long-lasting. At the same time, even if you have the most winning personality and an impeccable delivery, you won't truly have an influence on your listeners if you have nothing meaningful to say to them.

Working to create a successful speech must therefore take into account both of these crucial elements: the writing of the speech *and* your delivery of it. This book pays equal attention to both. The first part will take you step by step through the process of writing a speech, from coming up with ideas, to focusing on a topic, to polishing it to perfection. Following this procedure, you'll write a speech that clearly and effectively conveys the points that are important to you and that will interest your audience. This step-by-step process will also make certain you write a speech that will be as effective when spoken out loud as it is on the page.

The second part of the book addresses the many elements of delivering a speech. This section ensures that, having worked hard to write a perfect speech, you go on to deliver it in a manner that will effectively make a positive impression on your audience.

The third section includes samples of actual speeches. You can use them as models to give you ideas for writing your own successful speeches.

Whether you're about to give your first speech or have had some experience with public speaking and want to hone your skills, following these tips will enable you to make a speech that will leave your audience thinking, "What a natural."

Part I:

Writing Your Speech

1

Initial Considerations: Getting the Basic Information

> *A man surprised is half beaten.*
> —Dr. Thomas Fuller (1732)

The most successful speeches are those that are "custom-made," meaning they've been tailored to fit specific factors such as the composition of the audience and the type of event, occasion, and venue. When speeches aren't custom-made, they're just like bad, poorly tailored suits that simply don't "fit." They can seem sloppy, inappropriate, irrelevant, or generic, as if the speaker dusted off some old speech that's been lying around since the turn of the century. The audience, in turn, might be angry and resentful that the speaker clearly hasn't invested time in speaking specifically to them and meeting their expectations.

Just like a tailor who must first take extensive measurements before sewing a custom-made suit with a perfect fit, you also need to get a complete picture of the circumstances in which you'll be delivering your speech before you can begin writing it. So, before you rush out to consult your Encyclopedia of Quotations, even before you sharpen your pencil and start writing, it's extremely important that you take some time to ask questions and get basic information about the event and what is expected of you.

This chapter discusses these initial considerations, the issues and factors you need to devote some time to thinking about and then have in mind while writing your speech. At the end of the chapter you'll find a questionnaire to fill out to make certain you have gotten all the information you need to write a custom-made speech.

It's particularly important to address these considerations when you are an invited speaker who has been asked to address a group for a specific event or occasion (such as a convention or conference). In those instances, you'll have less control over the event and will want to work to meet whatever expectations the organizers have regarding the nature of your participation. There are of course many occasions when you might initiate your own speech. For example, you may call a meeting or organize an event at which you plan to speak yourself. In those cases, you'll be more aware than anyone of the purpose of your speech, but it's still worth it to think about the issues raised here. Even though you know your own purpose for speaking, you'll want to think about such factors as the audience to whom you are speaking and the expectations they might have.

Getting some of this information might require a bit of effort. You might have to make several phone calls and talk extensively with people involved in planning and organizing the event. When you are initially asked to speak, you'll have an opportunity to get a great deal of this information from whomever contacted you, and you should take advantage of it. Ask as many questions as you can based on the issues outlined below. At the same time, make certain you also get the name and phone number of a contact person you can call with additional questions and concerns as they arise. If this person is unable to help you, they might be able to put you in touch with someone who can.

These initial efforts will be worth the time as they'll enable you to write a better, more appropriate speech—and not be surprised by anything unexpected on the day you show up to speak in person.

BASIC INFORMATION: WHEN AND WHERE?

Start by making certain you know all the basics about when and where you will be speaking. That means the *exact* date, time, and address. As soon as you get this information, mark it on your calendar or datebook *immediately* so you won't forget it. This will also ensure you don't accidentally schedule yourself for something else on the same date.

When you mark the date on your calendar, also take note of how much time you have to prepare for the speech so you can budget your time accordingly. If you've got several weeks until the big day, you have enough time to carefully and methodically think about, plan, write, revise, and rehearse your speech. You also have enough time to conduct research and, if it is appropriate for your speech, create special "props" or supplemental materials to be presented and/or distributed to your audience (such as charts or slides). If time is short, you may have to forget about including these kinds of extras and instead concentrate more on writing and rehearsing the speech. You'll also have to plan on devoting more time each day to doing this.

If you have been asked to speak somewhere that involves having to travel, start investigating and making travel arrangements early on. This will not only help you get better fares and rates but will also ensure that you won't have a problem getting reservations. Find out if you are fully responsible for making and paying for your own arrangements, or if you can get assistance. If you have been invited to appear as a guest speaker by some organization, for example, some or all of your travel may be arranged and paid for by them. Similarly, if you are attending a convention or conference, the organizers may have arranged for discount travel and hotel fares.

WHAT IS THE PURPOSE OF YOUR SPEECH?

If you have been invited to speak by someone else, in addition to the basics of when and where you are going to give your speech, you should make certain you have a very clear idea of what you are supposed to discuss and why you were the one invited to speak. Occasionally you'll be given free rein and may speak about whatever you like. This usually is the case if the speaker is some well-known celebrity or expert, when just their presence is enough to get an audience interested regardless of the specific topic. Generally, however, you will be asked to speak for a very specific occasion to discuss some specific topic.

If you are initiating your own speech, you should still identify from the start the primary purpose for your speech. You don't want to take the time to gather people together to hear you and find you actually have nothing important to say.

There are many different purposes for giving speeches. But the main kinds of speeches generally fall into distinctive categories:

Storytelling

This is a speech in which you describe in detail (and usually in chronological order) some kind of experience you've had that will somehow influence or affect your listeners. It might, for example, be the story of how you achieved or accomplished something impressive, such as how you got a job or kicked smoking, or the story of how your company increased its profits.

Teaching

If you are an expert in some area you might be invited to share your knowledge in that field with others. Your speech in this case is a kind of lecture in which you are the teacher and the audience members are your students. A "teaching" speech might be instructing people how to use new equipment or computer software, or lecturing in your area of expertise, such as a particular academic or professional field.

Selling

In this instance, you give a speech in order to make a strong impression and convince your listeners to "buy" something. The most obvious example would be trying to get people to buy an actual product or services you offer, such as trying to win over new clients. However, you might also be "selling" something less tangible, such as a particular idea, argument, approach, or theory that you strongly advocate and want others to agree with. To inspire better morale, for example, you might speak to employees and "sell" them on the benefits of working harder and having a more positive attitude.

Problem Analysis/Solution

There's some problem, crisis or situation that you carefully assess in your speech and go on to offer a proposed solution. You are either an expert in the area and/or have done extensive research into this issue and can report your findings. For example, you might be discussing why your company's profits have suddenly declined. You take time to investigate the problem and in your speech describe factors that might be causing the decline and suggestions for turning it around.

Personal Homage

Many speeches involve talking in personal terms about the experiences and achievements of someone else and/or about your relationship with them. These speeches often take place on social occasions, such as milestone events like weddings, birthdays, and anniversaries, when you might be asked to give a toast. Even a roast is a kind of homage in which you poke fun at someone as a way of honoring them.

Personal homages are also sometimes given in the corporate world; more personal speeches are made, for example, to welcome new employees or honor those who are retiring.

In planning your speech, try to identify its purpose according to the above categories. This will help your planning and writing of the speech be more focused on a particular goal. Of course not all speeches will fit neatly into one of the above categories. However, these categories should give you a sense of reasons why speeches are often given and you can then figure out for yourself the specific purpose for the speech you have been invited and/or plan to give.

If it's not clear to you why you have been invited to speak or what topic you are supposed to discuss, it's fine for you to ask. Contact someone involved with the event (most likely the contact person who invited you), and say, "I'm just checking, is there anything specific that you'd like me to cover in my speech?"

WHAT IS EXPECTED OF YOU?

Even if you are fairly certain about the main purpose of your speech, it's a good idea to ask someone for more detailed information about what is expected of you. You might find that in addition to the overall topic, you are expected to speak about various subtopics or address certain questions. The event organizers might, for example, also want you to compile data and conduct research that you will present. They might be expecting you to prepare, present, and/or distribute special materials, such as handouts, brochures, slides, charts, or videotape footage.

You also might be expected to take a more active role in the proceedings in addition to speaking. For example, you might need to participate in a question-and-answer session with the audience or chair a panel. (More detailed descriptions of these various duties are included in Part II.) Find out early on if you are expected to play one of these special roles so that you can prepare for it.

WHAT IS THE OCCASION, EVENT OR VENUE?

Just as there are many types of speeches and varying purposes for them, there are also a variety of places and situations in which you might be speaking. Various occasions, events, and venues where speeches are often given include:

- conventions
- conferences
- seminars
- meetings (ranging in size from company-wide to departmental to committee)
- panel discussions
- parties
- breakfasts, luncheons, dinners, cocktail parties
- classrooms, lecture halls

Try to get as much specific information about the event, occasion, and venue as possible. It's helpful to know, for example, that you are speaking at a convention of advertisers, but it's even more helpful if you learn that the theme of this year's convention is "The Uses of Direct Marketing." That way you can gear your speech to the theme and focus of the convention. When asking about the purpose and expectations for your particular speech, also ask for details about the event. Ask to see any written materials describing the event, such as flyers, brochures, and advertisements. These materials might give you more insight into the nature of the event.

While you consider the event and occasion, also try to get more specific information about the circumstances and conditions in which you will be speaking. Are you one of many speakers who will be addressing an audience or are you the sole speaker? Will you sit alongside others on a panel or take turns going to the podium to speak individually? What kind of space will you be speaking in (such as a conference room, an auditorium, a catering hall, or a restaurant)? How many people does it hold? Is it equipped with audiovisual equipment? Will you need a microphone? Will you be speaking at a meal, such as a luncheon or cocktail party?

Try to get a very clear picture of the physical situation in which you will eventually be speaking. In some ways this will affect how you go about preparing for your speech. It will also cut down on any nervousness you might feel beforehand as you'll have a better sense of what to expect.

WHO IS YOUR AUDIENCE?

Good writing is always geared to a very specific audience in terms of content, style, and tone. For example, magazines are usually written in such a way as to appeal to a target readership; this target audience affects not only what is covered in the magazine but the way in which it is discussed. (*Teen People* and

Seventeen, for example, address topics and are written in a style that is completely different from *U.S. News and World Report*.)

For your speech to be successful, it must also speak very directly to your audience both in terms of content and style. To prepare a speech written for a particular audience, you must first have a very clear picture of who your audience is. If possible, try to get a sense of the composition of your audience in terms of:

- size
- age range
- gender
- profession
- educational level and background
- culture/religion/ethnicity
- social class
- experience, familiarity, expertise, and previous knowledge regarding your topic
- reason why they are attending the event in general and your speech in particular

Some of these traits might be more apparent than others. For example, if you are attending a conference or convention, the attendees will probably all have something obvious in common such as sharing the same profession or area of interest. However, it might still be difficult to assess other aspects of the audience such as their ages.

You should also be wary of making assumptions about a particular audience based solely on the topic or venue. For example, let's say you are invited to speak at a computer convention about new software you've developed. Assuming that those attending a computer convention will be well-versed in the field, you plan a speech written at a pretty sophisticated level. However, you arrive to find you are addressing retailers from a variety of stores; some know a great deal about computers, and some know nothing. It will be tough to change your speech on the spot to speak to this varied audience. Problematic situations like this can often be forestalled by asking questions and getting information in advance.

Probably the most important factor to assess is your audience's level of expertise and familiarity with your topic. You want to be able to speak to the audience on their level. If your entire audience is pretty knowledgeable about your field but you spend your speech defining terms they already know, they'll think you are talking down to them and become bored and resentful. On the other hand, if you presume they have a particular level of knowledge they actually do not possess and you then fail to define certain basic terms or concepts, you'll be speaking over their heads and lose them.

There are also many instances in which your audience will be diverse, composed of people from a variety of backgrounds with very different levels of experience. You will then have to write your speech more diplomatically, including enough to engage and interest everyone without necessarily alienating or confusing them.

You also want to get a very definite sense of how many people will be attending the speech as this will have an effect on the kind of speech you write. When you are speaking to a smaller audience, your speech can be more loosely structured and less scripted; you can take more time to talk directly to them and stop throughout to respond to questions or have more open discussions. When you are addressing a larger audience, though, you'll generally want a much more formal, carefully structured speech that is largely planned in advance.

HOW MUCH TIME?

It's also crucial that you find out how much time has been allocated for your speech. If a time limit has been set and announced for your speech, as is often the case when speeches are part of longer programs or events, then you must be careful to abide by it. If you go over the limit, people might have to leave in the middle of your speech because of other commitments or to attend other events. You might even be asked to end your speech before you are actually finished, and you won't then get to some of your most important points and powerful concluding statements. You also risk offending other speakers whose own time might be cut short if you go over your limit.

On the other hand, if you go under the announced, allotted time, there may be time left to kill, and people might feel disappointed that they didn't get the speech they were promised. Either way, going over or under is unprofessional and can disappoint whoever invited you to speak.

That's why it's so important that you be aware of the time limitation from the beginning. If you do know the amount of time set for your speech, you can write and edit it to fit the time. You won't then have to worry about being cut off in the middle or having to keep talking to kill time.

For some speeches, there might not be any time limitation, and it will be up to you to determine how long you would like to speak. The time factor is still something you should begin thinking about before writing your speech, although you do have more freedom to adjust it as you work on it. Have a ballpark figure in mind—some overall amount of time you think would be an appropriate length of time for your speech. Generally people prefer hearing speeches on the briefer side; nobody likes listening to someone yammer on too long, especially if no important points are being made. Frankly, few speeches ever need to take more than an hour as the absolute maximum, no matter what the purpose or occasion. Fifteen minutes is a good average figure for most speeches, although this does vary significantly depending on the purpose and type of speech. A fifteen-minute toast would seem unbearable (five minutes is more than sufficient), whereas fifteen minutes for a keynote address at a convention might seem far too short.

Even if the time is left to you, you might still want to talk to someone involved with the event to give you a ballpark figure for the overall amount of time that they feel would be appropriate for your speech. If you planned the event yourself, it's a good idea to tell people in advance how long you plan to speak. That way they can leave themselves enough time to listen to your entire speech without having to leave in the middle or watch the clock. They'll be more focused while you speak because they won't have to wonder when you'll finish.

QUESTIONNAIRE OF INITIAL CONSIDERATIONS

Before starting to write and plan your speech, take the time to complete the following questionnaire. You might have to make some phone calls or talk to people involved with the upcoming event to get this information. Once you fill out the entire questionnaire, you'll have all the information you need to begin writing your speech.

- When will the speech take place?
- Where will it take place?
- What is the exact date, time, and address?

- Do you need to make travel arrangements? Do the event organizers have any travel information or suggestions they can share with you?

- What is the event, venue, or occasion at which you will be speaking? Does it have a specific topic or theme?

- What is the overall purpose of your speech? Storytelling? Teaching? Selling? Analyzing a Problem? Personal Homage? Some other purpose?

- Why were you the one asked to give this speech? What are your qualifications for speaking on this subject?

- Do the organizers or planners have any specific expectations for what you will do or cover? Are there certain points or topics you are expected to cover during your speech? Are you expected to prepare any special kind of information or materials?

- Who will be in the audience? Will the audience members be similar in terms of background, age, gender, education, culture, social class, profession, and level of expertise? Or will they be more diverse? How familiar will most of them be with the field or subject your speech addresses?

- How many people are expected to attend your speech?

- What kind of room will you be speaking in? How big is it? What is its overall layout? Where will you be situated in relation to the rest of the audience? How many people can it hold? Will you need to use a microphone? Will one be provided for you?

- Will other people be speaking before or after you? Are you the only person who will be addressing the group or audience?

- How much time has been allotted for your speech?

- What will your exact role at the event be? Are you expected to do anything in addition to delivering your speech?

- Do you need to do any research or compile data? Do you want or need to prepare any props or special materials to present or distribute to the audience?

- If you plan on using any audiovisual equipment, how do you arrange for it to be supplied? Do you need to bring your own equipment? Is the room where you are speaking set up for audiovisual presentations?

- And always ask several times: Is there *anything* else expected of you?

2

Getting Ideas:
Percolating, Brainstorming,
Focusing on Key Points

*A man may die, nations may rise and fall, but
an idea lives on. Ideas have endurance without
death.*

—JOHN F. KENNEDY

*The best ideas caught him by surprise . . . when
his mind was elsewhere.*

—IAN MCEWAN, *AMSTERDAM*

A good speech is one that has something significant to say. That
may seem like an obvious point, but it's something that all too
many public speakers apparently forget. How many times have
you heard speakers giving speeches and thought to yourself,
"They're talking just to hear the sound of their own voice."
Speakers who just babble on without ever expressing anything
important, meaningful, or original leave an audience feeling frustrated, as if their time has been wasted.

The speakers who impress listeners, on the other hand, are the
ones who show they've given their topic a great deal of thought.
You can tell they've thought about their topic because the speech
itself makes important points and expresses interesting and
original *ideas*.

It takes time and effort to generate ideas for a speech. For that
reason, you can't expect to sit down and start writing a speech

without first giving it some careful thought. After you've identified the important initial considerations discussed in the last chapter, give yourself time to let ideas *percolate*. Then work more actively on *brainstorming*.

PERCOLATION TIME

Great ideas don't come to us on demand; we can't force ourselves to come up with them on the spot no matter how hard we try. In fact, forcing ideas to come often disrupts the creative process, leading to a feeling of being blocked. However, after we give ourselves some time to mull over something for awhile, giving our thoughts about a particular project a chance to percolate, then they come through loud and clear, like a cup of strongly brewed coffee.

Now that you've identified your speech's purpose and thought about such factors as the occasion and audience, you need to give yourself that time to let your mind go to work. The best way to encourage your brain to begin generating ideas is to give it a little freedom and not try to force it too hard. You'll find that as you go about your daily routine, ideas will begin to pop into your head, even if you're not necessarily concentrating hard on your upcoming speech. Suddenly, though, you'll realize you've got an idea about something you'd like to say, a point you think would be worth making when you speak.

Certain activities we do every day can work particularly well as effective "thinking times." These are those daily routines that require little concentration, leaving our minds free to wander and helping our creative juices to flow—such as the morning routine of showering and getting dressed, going to the gym and working out, even riding the bus or train. You can also add activities to your daily routine to give you more "thinking time" such as taking long walks or sitting still listening to your favorite music.

Get in the habit of carrying around a small notebook with you so that you can keep track of ideas as they come to you. You don't have to worry about writing clear, complete sentences. Just jot down a few phrases so that you won't forget these ideas. Note *all* ideas related to your speech as they occur to you, even if you aren't entirely certain how strong they are or if they will work well in your speech. Write them all down as they come to you, and you can worry later about which ones are the best and most appropriate points to make.

IMMERSION THERAPY

In addition to giving yourself "thinking time" to let ideas percolate, you can also try immersing yourself more thoroughly in the subject matter. You should be able to identify at least one, or even several, broad subject areas related to your speech. By becoming more immersed in these areas, you'll increase the amount of time you spend thinking about the speech and give yourself more opportunity to come up with ideas.

This immersion process need not be an arduous task. It does not have to nor should it involve conducting intensive research and taking meticulous notes to be incorporated into the speech. (Many speeches do, though, require research, which is discussed in the next chapter.) Instead, there are many ways you can casually become more involved with your subject in a way that is fun and informative.

Reading materials related to your subject is a good starting place. You might choose to consult an encyclopedia or almanac, just to be able to read a broad overview of your subject. There are also many specialty encyclopedia and reference works available in the library, in which you might find more detailed information about more specific topics. Ask the librarian to make suggestions for you. Don't be intimidated about asking the librarians for help. That's their job, and most will be happy to give you suggestions. Tell them the subject of your speech and see if they have ideas for interesting sources. You might also go the bookstore or library and find the section in which books related to your subject are shelved in order to find various sources to examine.

As you find these various reading materials, you don't necessarily need to read them cover to cover. Just flip through them casually, skimming sections that seem of interest, or looking closely at anything in particular that catches your eye.

In addition to reading about the subject, you might find other ways to become more immersed in it. Perhaps there are films or television shows that you might watch on videotape. You might also visit particular locations related to the topic, such as museums.

The Internet is a particularly valuable, easily accessible resource. If you have Internet access, try surfing the Web a bit. Do a search using words related to your subject as key words and see what turns up. If you don't know how to use the Internet, you might ask a friend to help you. It's easy to do and fun.

Any way that you can think of to focus your thoughts more on your speech's subject area(s) will be useful. Even if you are very familiar with the subject, it won't hurt for you to refamiliarize yourself with it for a short period before you begin writing. Just remember to keep documenting any ideas that pop into your head during this immersion period.

TALKING THROUGH IDEAS

In addition to giving yourself thinking time and immersing yourself in the subject, you may find it helpful to talk with other people about it. Tell a few people who are close to you that you will be giving a speech on a particular topic and share some of your thoughts with them. Encourage them in turn to ask you questions about the topic. Based on what they ask you and your response, you may find you come up with even more ideas. Talking through an idea with someone else can help you identify and better focus your own thoughts. Sometimes random ideas will be floating around inside your head, not fully developed, and you just haven't made the extra effort yet to articulate them. A conversation with someone else though can help that to happen. Again, after talking though these ideas with someone, take the time to jot down thoughts in your notebook so you won't forget them.

BRAINSTORMING

After giving yourself a few days to let ideas percolate, you need then to begin more actively generating and compiling them. You can do that by brainstorming—a process in which you focus exclusively on the task of coming up with ideas about a topic in a focused, organized fashion.

The best way to brainstorm ideas is to sit with some blank pieces of paper in front of you and free write. Free writing, as the name implies, means writing down whatever pops into your head, without worrying about grammar, punctuation, or formality. This writing is for your eyes only, so you don't need to worry about how much sense it makes to other readers. When you sit down to brainstorm, free write about the topic or subject areas for your speech. Write down whatever thoughts and images come into your mind. You can also rewrite the ideas you have been writing down in your notebook or that had been running through your mind during your percolation time.

As the word "brainstorming" indicates, ideas might come to you in a storm-like fashion. At times, you'll be *flooded* with them. At others, you may not come up with anything. The ideas will also come to you in a random, chaotic fashion. That's okay, though. These are just the fine strands that will at some point be woven into a more polished final product. Like an artist, you first need to gather all the materials and examine them before you can use them to create your finished work.

If time allows, you may want to have several brainstorming sessions. Give yourself a break between them to give your mind a rest. Coming back with a clear head gives you an opportunity for a fresh start. Try to begin each new free writing session by reading over your notes from the last one. That often will be enough to jumpstart the brainstorming process, sparking some new idea that will get you writing more.

IDENTIFY KEY POINTS

Now you've given your subject matter thought, and spent time just letting thoughts percolate in your mind. You've immersed yourself in your subject matter, and perhaps talked to others about it. Most recently, you've brainstormed, putting whatever ideas occur to you on paper.

You may be pleasantly surprised to see you've generated a tremendous amount of material. However, it won't be possible for you to include all of this in your speech, and many of it may not even be all that appropriate or necessary for your speech. So before going on to the process of actually writing the speech, you need to take time to review and evaluate all these ideas, and select the best to be included in the speech.

Read over all the notes you've been taking, ask yourself these questions, and highlight all parts of your notes that apply:

- Which ideas are the most original ones that will most impress and interest my audience?
- Which ideas are important to me? Which are the ones I really want to tell other people about?

Next, take those highlighted sections and rewrite those ideas on a separate piece of paper. As you do, try rewriting them in a more coherent manner that would in fact be understandable to another reader.

When you now examine these ideas on one sheet of paper, you might start to notice that some are very closely related while others stray from the topic. As you notice this, try grouping similar ideas together. Ones that can't be categorized together are probably worth eliminating. They may be interesting ideas in their own right, but they probably won't generate enough material for a whole speech. You want your finished speech to remain tightly focused on a single topic. It's therefore important that the points your raise within the speech be very closely connected.

Now, examine the list once again and circle or highlight the ideas that you think are the most important. Try to include *no more than five*. These will serve as your key talking points. They are the ideas you feel are absolutely crucial to express in your speech.

This does not mean that all the other ideas you noted won't come into the speech. As you are writing, you might find they do in fact need to be included. You might also find some are irrelevant and can be left out. However, the key points are the ones you do want to make certain you address.

WHAT'S THE MAIN IDEA?

Having identified your key points, the next and most important part of this whole process is identifying the speech's main idea or theme. In the last chapter, you thought about the speech's purpose, perhaps to tell a story or analyze a problem. Now, you need to identify a more specific, focused point you especially want to express to your audience, or a clearly defined theme you want to concentrate on. Ask yourself, "What is the one thing I most want my audience to learn from me, the one thing I most want them to remember, the one impression I most want to make?" This main idea/theme might be one of the key points you've already listed that you deem the most important. You might, on the other hand, find yourself only now coming up with a main idea/theme based on all this thought you've put into preparing for the speech.

Once you've identified the main idea, write it out in clear block letters and keep it close at hand, along with the key points, as you plan and write the speech. You've put a lot of time and effort into coming up with these key points, but you'll find it was time well spent. You'll find this process will actually make writing and editing the speech much easier. They'll serve as guideposts while you write your speech, ensuring you stay focused on what's important and that these meaningful ideas become central components of your speech. Your audience is then certain to appreciate the thought that went into your speech, and know that your speech, unlike all too many others, does have something meaningful and important to say.

3

Gathering Information: What Kind of Information Do You Need to Include in Your Speech?

If the blind lead the blind, both shall fall into the ditch.
—BIBLICAL PROVERB

It is terrible to speak well and be wrong.
—SOPHOCLES, *ELECTRA*

WHY DO RESEARCH FOR A SPEECH?

A good speaker is a well-informed one; a good speech conveys accurate information about a particular topic. When you give a speech, you need to think of yourself as an expert in whatever subject area you are speaking. You may already be an expert in that area, which is often why you have been invited to speak in the first place. If you're not an expert, though, you need to make yourself one in order to write and deliver the speech. Take time to study up on the subject so that your speech conveys accurate information and you can speak with authority. By making yourself well informed, you also will be better prepared to answer questions following the speech.

In addition to generally wanting to make yourself better informed of the subject, you also might need to conduct research in order to gather information to include in your speech. As we saw in the last chapter, one of the main purposes of a speech is to communicate your ideas regarding a particular subject. However, a large portion of a speech also consists of sharing pieces of information culled from other sources that illustrate or support these ideas. When your ideas are supported by this kind of evidence, they're stronger and more compelling; rather than being mere opinions that you force on the audience, they become valid views that you've shown to be well documented and accurate.

INFORMATION CATEGORIES

There are several basic categories of information included in a speech:

Your Own Knowledge

Presumably there is a reason why you were asked to speak or chose to speak on a particular topic, and that is that you already have some degree of knowledge about that subject. You can certainly draw on your previous knowledge of a subject in a speech, provided that you are certain it is factually correct.

Before beginning a more formal research process, sit down with blank sheets of paper and jot down whatever you know already regarding the subject. Unlike the brainstorming process in the last chapter in which you generated ideas, concentrate now on writing down the factual knowledge you possess that illustrates or supports those ideas. If you find your knowledge regarding a particular piece of information is a bit shaky, you might want to consult some other sources.

In those speeches in which it is crucial that you convince your audience of the validity of your argument (such as "selling" speeches), you might want to supplement your knowledge with additional material from other sources. By including additional sources, you create a stronger argument, indicating that your ideas are well supported in a number of ways.

Factual Information from Outside Sources

Much of a speech consists of presenting facts, although those facts might be used in a number of ways. They can be presented to an audience as part of a "teaching" speech in which you share new information with them about a particular subject that they have no previous knowledge of. They also might serve as "evidence" to support your ideas, theories, and arguments, as in "selling" speeches in which you are trying to convince the audience to buy or do something.

You'll see below that there are a variety of sources from which you can gather this information. In "selling" speeches, you generally want to choose sources that are up-to-date and reputable. By choosing the more contemporary sources, your speech becomes more timely, which will lend it greater relevance to your audience. By choosing reputable sources, you build a stronger argument for yourself. For example, citing a story from a major newspaper like the *New York Times* or *Wall Street Journal* would probably be more impressive to your audience than quoting from a supermarket tabloid.

Quotations/Paraphrases

Very often, speakers choose to quote or paraphrase someone else on something relevant to whatever point they are trying to make. (A quotation is an *exact retelling* of whatever someone else said, while a paraphrase is an *accurate summary* of what the person originally said.) You'll see in Chapter 6, "Saying It with Style" that including quotations is an effective strategy for making a speech sound more interesting, as it helps make the writing more varied.

In addition to adding variety to your speech, they provide an opportunity for you to bring other people's ideas, opinions, and theories into your speech. You might refer to these ideas as a way to support your own. You also might introduce opinions that differ from yours so that you can argue against them, thereby making your views sound stronger.

For quotations to be effective, though, they need to be very well-said and/or drawn from a source that will impress your audience. If neither of these qualities applies, the quotation probably is too boring, generic, or irrelevant to be worthy of inclusion. The quotations should add something meaningful to your speech and not merely repeat factual information that can be culled from any number of sources.

Statistics and Data

Statistical evidence and data drawn from various studies or experiments provide a particular kind of factual information that can be very powerful in a speech. Numerical findings and percentages give scientific support for your ideas that is difficult to refute.

However, you should only bring up statistics and data that come from reputable sources. The studies or experiments from which these numbers are drawn should be conducted by unbiased professionals or experts in the field who work under carefully controlled conditions to produce accurate results.

If you discover some kind of statistical evidence or data you wish to include in your speech, keep in mind that you'll need to make it understandable and relevant to your audience. If you merely quote the findings, you'll just be listing numbers, which are difficult for an audience to concentrate on. However, if you take those numbers and make it clear how they support or relate to the point you are making, you'll be using the statistics in a way that enables your audience to appreciate their relevance. That means you need to make certain you fully understand what the statistics indicate before you can share them with an audience. Take the time to read all studies, experiments, and reports that include statistics and data very carefully so that you fully understand them yourself and can then present them clearly to others.

WHERE TO FIND IT

Based on the specific purpose of your speech, you should have a sense of how much additional information you need to include beyond your own knowledge. Most "selling," "teaching," and problem analysis" speeches require you to draw heavily on information from other sources to support, illustrate, and document your ideas, opinions, and theories. "Storytelling" and "personal homages" often can consist of your own knowledge and experiences, although you occasionally might want to include some information from other sources (such as famous quotations).

Having identified what kind of information you need to find, you now need to conduct research in order to get it. These are some of the best places to gather information:

Books, Magazines, Journals

The primary way people research a topic is to turn to written source materials—books, magazines, and journals. To track down relevant materials of this nature, go to a bookstore or library and search by subject. In a bookstore, you should be able to find a section where those books related to your subject are shelved.

Libraries shelve books according to an even wider range of categories and probably have many more sources for you to consult. When you go to the library, try doing a search in the subject catalog. You only need find one book related to your subject in the catalog; when you find that book in the library, it will be shelved with other books on the same subject. You can then scan the section to find any books that seem specifically relevant to your speech.

You can also ask the reference librarian for help. As suggested in the last chapter, don't be afraid to tell the librarian what your speech is about and ask for suggestions about possible source materials. They might provide you with specific sources, or point out specialized indexes and bibliographies related to your topic that list possible sources. At the very least, they can point you in the right direction within the library.

The Internet

Thanks to the Internet, you can get a wealth of information without having to leave your home or office. Try surfing the Web, using key words related to your subject as the basis for a search. When you get to a helpful site, you can follow links that will take you to other related sites.

The advantage to using the Internet for research is the ease with which you can track down a great deal of material, but there are a few drawbacks. For one, it's difficult to read and take notes on information from a computer screen, and printing out material is time consuming. Another problem is that much material written for the Internet is deliberately succinct, to make for easier reading. As a result, you may not get the same kind of detailed information you need to have a fully informed speech. However, the Internet can certainly be an excellent starting place for your research; depending on the purpose for your speech, you may get all you need from it without necessarily needing to turn to other sources.

In addition to the Internet, there may be CD-ROMs available that relate to your subject. Go to a computer store and ask the clerk if there are any on the market that you might find useful.

Company Files/Office Library

If you are working on a speech related to your business, you may be able to rely heavily on your company's own resources. Many companies keep detailed files on subjects related to their type of business, and some even have their own libraries, which have books, magazines, and other materials related to the field. Before running out to a bookstore or public library, find out what kind of information is more readily available to you from your own office.

Interviews

In trying to make yourself an expert on a particular subject, you might consider interviewing other experts in the field, or anyone who has specific information you need or possesses a better understanding of a particular topic than you do. These people might impart information you can present in your speech (and attribute to them), or suggest other possible sources you might consult.

Interviews can be a particularly vital research tool for preparing personal homages, especially when you are speaking about someone whom you don't know well. In these instances, you can interview people who do know the honoree and relate what they had to say in your speech. You make yourself an "expert" on the honoree by talking to the "experts" who know them best.

Dictionaries/Encyclopedias of Quotations

It's very easy to track down quotations, as there are so many compilations of them available. You can go to a bookstore or the reference section of a library and flip through any number of books that collect various quotations.

Some compilations of quotations bring together quotations of all kinds, while others center on specific topics, such as humorous quotations or contemporary references. To make the research process easier, you might consider consulting books that are organized by topic rather than speaker. That means you can simply scan the list of topics, looking for any that relate to your subject, and then read all the quotes listed beneath those topics. When books are organized by person, you need to check the index for possible topics, and then flip around through the book to find them, which can be a tedious process. However, if you know of a specific quote you want to track down in order to get the exact wording, you might find it more useful to search through a book organized by the speakers' names.

HOW TO USE IT

After you track down sources, you need to gather information from them for possible incorporation in your speech. Read through the materials and take notes on anything that you think will be relevant to specific areas of your speech, particularly anything that documents or illustrates various ideas and points you are trying to communicate.

You might consider taking notes on index cards. Each card can focus on one specific piece of information. You can note on it the place in your speech where you think it would best apply. As you take notes, you can then group together cards that relate to the same idea or key point. This kind of organized notetaking will make it easier when you sit down to write your speech, as you will have the information on hand without having to flip through stacks and stacks of papers.

Some (and maybe even most) of this information may not eventually come into your finished speech. You'll only want to introduce information into your speech that strongly supports what you have to say or is clearly relevant to some point you want to make. You don't want to include so much information from outside sources that it overwhelms your speech and your ideas get lost. Your voice should come through loudest and clearest.

When you conduct research, though, it's fine to take lots of notes, even if you won't ultimately use it all. By taking notes now, you give yourself more options about what to include later on when you write the speech. For example, when you look up quotations related to your topic, copy down several of them that you find interesting or clever. When you get to writing your speech, you can then choose the ones you think work best.

Additionally, by conducting this research, you are generally making yourself more knowledgeable about the subject, which will help give you a stronger, more authoritative presentation. Information not included in a speech may be helpful to you during a question-and-answer session following the interview.

As you take notes, make certain you clearly indicate to yourself the source that each bit of information comes from. Some of this you might have to cite in your speech. Any piece of information that is not a well-known, substantiated fact should be attributed to whatever source you culled it from within the speech.

Additionally, you might find that after a speech, people in the audience would like to know more about the subject and ask you for suggestions about other source materials. You should always bring a complete list of sources with you to a speech, even if they weren't directly referred to in the final speech.

A WORD ON AUDIOVISUAL PROPS AND SPECIAL MATERIALS

Audiovisual props such as slides, charts, graphs, and video clips can be highly effective ways to illustrate certain points of a speech. For example, in addition to quoting statistics, you can show a graph or chart that illustrates them. If you are trying to win over a new client to your advertising agency, you might show them examples of the advertising campaigns you've created. In some instances, your audiences will be expecting you to present some kind of special material like this to them, which is something you should find out early on in planning your speech.

These special props provide an audience with images that are easier to focus upon than the spoken word and more likely to be remembered later on. By giving a speech greater variety, adding an element in addition to the spoken voice, they tend to be attention-getters that inspire audiences to concentrate even more on what you have to say.

More detailed instructions on how to prepare and utilize these kinds of materials are outlined in Part II: Delivering Your Speech. As you now conduct research, though, you might want to keep your eyes open for any material that particularly lends itself to some form of visual presentation.

4

Planning an Effective Strategy: The Three-Part Speech Format

Make no little plans: they have no magic to stir men's blood.

—DANIEL H. BURNHAM

You've now spent a fair amount of time brainstorming ideas, determining your key points and main idea, and gathering information. As a result, you now most likely have a great deal that you'd like to talk about in your speech. There are many ways in which your ideas and research can be presented, and before you can begin writing, you need to make decisions about the most effective way to do so.

You can't simply discuss ideas and raise points and pieces of information in a random fashion, skipping from one topic to another. That would only serve to confuse and annoy your audience. You therefore want your ideas to be presented in an orderly, clear manner so that they easily make sense to the audience. That's one reason why, before writing, you should take time to think about the *way* you are going to present information in the speech.

There's more to giving an effective speech, though, than presenting ideas *clearly*. You also want your speech to have *impact*, to have some kind of an effect or influence on the audience. Perhaps you want to move or inspire them. You might want them to be impressed with your ideas and learn something from you. Maybe you want to motivate them to take some kind of action, perhaps persuading them to buy or do something. In addition to wanting your whole speech to have a particular effect on your audience, there are also certain points you probably want them to make note of and take away with them.

To have this kind of impact on an audience, you need to think of your speech in *strategic terms*. Planning a speech is somewhat similar to what military leaders do before going into battle— carefully assessing the situation and creating a plan of attack that will best use their resources to ensure a victory. Similarly, before attorneys go to court, they examine their evidence and select which pieces to use and which witnesses to question on the stand. They also decide on the order in which to present this evidence, knowing that this has a profound effect on how the jury interprets it. You need to plan your speech with similar strategic considerations in mind.

That's why the last step before you sit down and begin writing the first draft of your speech is to plan an effective strategy. This strategy will determine the order in which you will discuss your ideas, share the information you've gathered in your research, and raise your key points.

This chapter describes a three-part format that you can use to structure any speech you give. This format, as you'll see, is the clearest, most organized way to present material to an audience, guaranteeing they'll be able to follow your discussion and focus on your main points and ideas. It's also designed to engage your audience's attention, guaranteeing that your most important points have the kind of impact that separates a forgettable speech from a great one.

The three parts of an effective speech consist of:

- **The Opening**, including a *hook* to grab the audience's attention and introduce the *main idea/theme* of your speech, as well as a *preview* of what you will discuss in the rest of the speech
- **The Body,** including a detailed discussion of your various ideas and key points, presented in an order that makes sense for the given topic and is strategically effective; and

- **Closing Remarks,** including a brief *review* of your key points and the main idea/theme, as well as your *final thoughts* that you want the audience to take away with them.

This chapter discusses each part of this format in detail. You should read this chapter carefully and make certain you understand this format before you sit down to write. As you'll see here, you need to make various decisions about what to include in each part of your speech and think about the most effective way to present that information in each section. Tips to help you make those choices—and ensure your speech affects your audience the way you want it to—are also discussed here.

THE OPENING

They say that most moviegoers make a decision about whether or not they like a particular movie within the first five minutes, and that initial decision influences their mood and level of attention for the entire film. Speeches are no different. In the first few minutes, you'll either grab the audience's attention and have them eager to follow your words for the duration, or you'll lose them and have little chance of recapturing their interest.

We like to believe that first impressions lie. That's often proven true in those instances when we have multiple opportunities to interact with someone and get to know them better than we did on a first meeting. However, when you give a speech, the first impression is usually the only impression your audience will get of you and your ideas. That's why those first few minutes of a speech are crucial, and you must make certain you use them effectively.

If that sounds like it's putting a lot of pressure on your speech's opening, it should. You should think about your opening very carefully. Preparing it might even take more time and effort than the rest of your speech. That's okay, though, because the opening is that important.

Like the entire speech, there are several parts to an effective opening: the *hook*, the *main idea/theme*, and the *preview*. Including all of these elements ensures that you grab the audience's attention right from the start while giving them a clear idea of your speech's specific focus. In this way, you make a positive first impression on your listeners and put them on a solid path that leads right to the body of your speech.

THE HOOK AND THE MAIN IDEA/THEME

To capture the audience's attention, you should start your speech with a hook—something that will take hold of your audience and help you draw them into the body of your speech. The hook should be something that has a strong, dramatic impact on the audience, capturing their imaginations, intriguing them, getting them thinking, or even surprising them. Most importantly, it should succeed in getting every audience member's attention focused on you; they should now be waiting on your every word.

That's not the only purpose of the opening, though. It's also extremely important that you use it to introduce the main idea/theme of your speech that you defined in Chapter 2. The audience needs a very clear idea of what your speech will be about early on. Knowing the speech's main idea/theme gives them something to concentrate on while they listen. They'll be able to see that the points and pieces of information you are raising throughout are connected to this larger idea. They'll also appreciate knowing that there's a greater purpose at work that you've given time and thought to, that you've got a reason for sharing this information.

The hook therefore has to grab the audience's attention but also lead to the main idea/theme. You might be able to start a speech with a really great opening, but if it doesn't clearly lead into the rest of the speech, it's pointless. In fact, it might confuse and even anger your audience. In this case, rather than a hook, you've got a hammer—an opening that hits the audience on the head with some kind of striking image or statement, but ultimately goes nowhere. Rather than continuing to draw them further into the speech the way a hook would, a hammer leaves them feeling dazed and confused, with a bit of a headache.

Examples

An Opener with a Hammer:

According to today's paper, a major earthquake is going to hit this area within the next ten years. If it hits today, we're all certain to be killed. Hopefully, that won't happen during my speech, which is about how to decrease our spending and increase our profits.

An Opener with a Hook:

"Major Earthquake Likely to Hit Within the Next Ten Years." That was a headline in today's paper and, if you're like me, you saw it and felt tempted to panic. Fortunately, before I began packing all of my bags and sold my house, I read the rest of the article. This headline, it turns out, was based on a single study that many other scientists are disputing, and the likelihood of the earthquake hitting was actually only a three in ten chance. Moreover, such an earthquake would probably only cause minor damage, most of which could be decreased or prevented if we make the proper advanced preparations.

My reaction to this headline made me think about the danger of acting on a gut emotional response without taking time to think. In any bad situation, we need to fight off the temptation to panic, and instead assess the situation and deal with it. That's certainly the way we need to respond to the losses we took this quarter, which is what I want to talk about today.

Do you see how the first example will no doubt get people's attention but has nothing to do with the actual topic of the speech? How do you think the audience will react to this opening?

On the other hand, look at how smoothly the second example uses the hook to lead to the main idea/theme of the speech.

TYPES OF HOOKS

Here are several suggestions for openings that will hook your audience. No matter which one you use, though, it is imperative that it do these two things:

1. Grab your audience's attention
2. Draw your audience further into your speech by leading to the main idea/theme

1. Share a Short Story, Anecdote, or Personal Experience

Remember when you were a kid and it was story time? Did you beg to hear one more story or another chapter before going to bed? Do you remember how hearing well-told stories captured your imagination and made you want to hear more?

Even as adults, people love to hear stories. Stories easily engage our attention with vivid images and make us want to hear more from the storyteller. Those are all things you want your audience to experience during your speech's opening. That's why telling a story or anecdote often makes for a dramatic and extremely effective hook.

There are several kinds of stories you might tell. You might describe an interesting experience that happened to you or someone you know. You might relate an amusing or interesting anecdote that you read or overheard somewhere. You could describe a scene in a popular movie, book, or play. You might even tell an entirely fictitious story that you made up for the occasion or read somewhere.

The key, as with all the hooks, is making the story lead clearly into the rest of the speech. Try to choose a story or anecdote that illustrates a principle crucial to your speech. This will ensure there is a firm connection between the opening hook and the rest of the speech. To make certain that connection is apparent to the audience, you can follow the story or anecdote by telling them exactly how it leads to or illustrates your speech's main idea. You simply need to say something like: "This shows us. . . " or "That experience taught me. . . ."

It's also important that the story be an interesting one and that you tell it well. An advantage to starting a speech by telling a story is that it gives you an opportunity to describe an event using vivid details. Use highly descriptive words to set the scene, characterize the people involved, and play up any drama or action involved. In so doing, you use language to paint a picture the audience can easily focus on. They'll also get an impression that you are a good orator, that you know how to use words to effectively communicate powerful images and ideas to them. They'll look forward to hearing what else you have to tell them.

Example of Telling a Story as a Hook

The first time I met the woman who would become my wife, she was interviewing for the same job I was. We talked for a while in the reception area, and I knew she was someone special. But I was too shy to ask for her phone number, something for which I cursed myself the whole way home and for many months afterward. A year later, I saw her on a subway platform. This time, I vowed I wouldn't be too timid. I struck up a conversation; fortunately she remembered me, and then I asked her out for coffee. She thanked me and told me she was going to meet her boyfriend. So it was not to be, I thought, or at least it seemed that way at the time. Well, I thought about her all the time. And sure enough, I ran into her again about six months later in a bookstore. And again, I asked her out for coffee. This time, she said yes. It turned out she had ditched the boyfriend months ago. Two years after that first date, we were married. That, more than anything else, showed me the value of perseverance, which is the theme of my talk today. Perseverance worked for me personally, but it also can be a crucial asset professionally. Let me explain what I mean.

2. Begin with a Contemporary Reference

Another way to attract an audience's interest in your speech is to start with some kind of contemporary reference. This means raising a topic, issue, or event that relates to something going on right here and now. Such timely references lend a speech greater immediacy, relevance, and importance, speaking more directly to the audience's current experiences and concerns.

For example, look at this opening for a speech that uses a non-contemporary reference:

> In Ancient Greece, plays were presented as parts of elaborate festivals in which awards were given for the best comedy, tragedy, and actors. Even back then, competition was a central part of life, and artists were branded winners and losers. Today, competition is still a part of life for us, even in business.

The following speech, on the other hand, uses a more contemporary reference to introduce the same topic:

> Did you all watch the Oscars last night? Did you see the look on Lauren Bacall's face when she lost? Just like everybody watching, she thought she was certain to win. And when they read out someone else's name, she actually showed her surprise and disappointment. In a way, I found it admirable. She was having a purely emotional response, without the kind of hypocritical display most other people put on. At the same time, I couldn't help thinking that my fascination with the Oscars has more to do with seeing how the losers respond than with learning who actually wins. There's something comforting about seeing people we admire

losing a competition, grappling with an adverse situation that we too often have to deal with ourselves. Losing is a part of life, for celebrities and for all of us. It's something we also must learn how to grapple with in the business world.

Even though the first example is somewhat interesting, the second one with the reference to the Oscars would probably better draw in the audience because it introduces a more contemporary event that more people in the audience can relate to.

There are several kinds of contemporary references you might use as your opening hook:

News Stories: Look through newspapers and magazines for current news stories that can somehow be tied to your speech. They might be big stories currently making headlines, or lesser known news items that are nevertheless interesting. Just make certain they are relevant to your speech.

Current Events: As the Oscars example shows, you need not bring up a news story but can discuss any kind of well-known current event. Look at events happening right now, or that recently took place, or that will take place in the next few days. You can refer to events taking place in the same vicinity as your speech, or ones in other locations. If the event is taking place somewhere else, make certain it's one that everyone will know about and find interesting.

On the other hand, you might refer to an event taking place in or near the site where you are delivering your speech (such as something happening in the same city, town, or office building). In fact, the closer the event is to the site of your speech, the more it will be of interest to your audience. It will also make them feel good that you are speaking about something more directly related to them.

The Physical Location: In addition to choosing to describe events taking place near or around the site of your speech, there may be something interesting about the physical location itself you want to discuss. Perhaps the site has an interesting history or distinguishing feature (such as a mural or piece of sculpture) you can refer to and somehow use to introduce your speech.

Refer to the Occasion or Venue: You can also refer more directly to the occasion at which you are speaking, especially if there is something special or unique about it. For example, if you are speaking at a conference or convention, there might be a specific focus or theme to it that year, or it might be held in honor of someone's memory, or even be a milestone event, such as the twenty-fifth annual convention of its kind. Those are the kinds of distinctive elements you could use to create a timely hook that has special meaning for your audience.

A Contemporary Trend: If there's some hot topic or trend that's currently very popular, you might use it as a hook. You might mention a popular movie or TV show that many people are currently watching, or a hot trend that everyone's into. This can often enable you to have a more humorous, entertaining opening.

The Date: If your speech falls on a special date, such as a holiday or milestone occasion, you can refer to it at the start of your speech. You'll have to get creative, though, in finding something to say about that date and relate it to your speech. You can't begin by saying "Today is April 15" and then move on to another topic of discussion. Everyone in the audience will know what day it is. You need instead to say something about the significance of that date that will connect it with your speech.

3. Cite a Famous Quotation

In many ways, the easiest way to come up with an opening hook is to start out with a quotation. It's not all that hard to find a good quotation that relates to your topic. You can, as discussed in the last chapter, examine dictionaries or encyclopedias of quotations. Use the index to look up your topic or topics closely related to the subject of your speech and see if you find any quotations related to it that you like.

The problem with this kind of opening, though, is that it has become too commonplace. Audiences often expect a speech to start off with a quotation, and when they then hear you begin with one, even if it's a really good one, they might not be as interested as they would be by hearing something totally unexpected.

However, that doesn't necessarily mean you can't open with a quotation at all. If none of these other suggestions for hooks work, or if you don't have much time to think about and plan your speech, this can be a fine opening tactic. Just make certain that you do in fact choose a really juicy quotation that will grab people's attention. Avoid quotations that are so famous they are now clichés. Also, it's usually more effective to quote someone familiar to most of the audience. If you quote someone they've never heard of, chances are they won't care what this person had to say, no matter how well he or she said it.

This is one reason why you need to have a clear picture of who your audience is as you write your speech. For example, if you are addressing a group of scientists, they will be familiar with certain people that the general public might not be. They won't mind you quoting Stephen Hawking, for example, as they will likely have heard of him and value whatever he has to say. On the other hand, if you are speaking to an audience largely unfamiliar with him, his name will be meaningless. When you start out saying, "Stephen Hawking once said," their reaction will be, "Who?" and even more problematic, "Who cares?"

Consider too that the type of quotation you pick will have a specific impact on the audience. Quotations can be witty, humorous, scathing, illuminating, thought-provoking, surprising, startling, inspiring—and the audience's response will reflect the kind of quotation you choose. Use a quotation appropriate for your topic that will put the audience in the right frame of mind for the rest of your speech.

Examples of a Quotation as a Hook

"Everybody on this planet is separated by only six people. Six degrees of separation. Between us and everybody else on this planet. The president of the United States. A gondolier in Venice. Fill in the names." That's a quotation from one of my favorite plays, *Six Degrees of Separation* by John Guare. I always find that speech incredibly moving and yet thought-provoking. If we're connected to everyone on the planet by only six people, think about the even closer connections we have here within our company, or with our clients. Thinking about those connections makes me wonder about how the things we do as individuals have more widespread consequences, affecting far more people than we realize. Today, I want to examine some of these widespread consequences of our daily business practices, and identify ways in which we can ensure they lead to positive outcomes.

4. Tell a Joke or Humorous Story

Many people have the idea that all good speeches must start with some kind of joke. In a way this thinking makes sense. You tell a joke and, if you get people laughing, they're clearly getting something from the speech. You put them in a good mood, entertain them, and get them to like you, as if you were a class clown or party host. That all sounds great, right? Well, not necessarily.

First of all, just because you are entertaining the audience doesn't mean you're really having an impact on them. The purpose for many speeches is often to do something more serious than amuse your audience. For some speeches, humor might even be inappropriate and considered in bad taste, particularly if you are discussing a very serious topic.

Another problem with this kind of opening is that you take a big risk—the joke might always die. You might think a certain joke is hilarious, only to find when you tell it in front of an audience, or in front of this particular audience, that no one finds it at all funny. Then you'll have to deal with an awkward silence that gets the speech off on an uncertain footing, making it harder for you to continue speaking feeling good about what you have to say.

Finally, perhaps the most serious problem with starting a speech with a joke is that it's done so often it has become somewhat of a cliché. It therefore won't have the impact that a more unexpected or innovative opening might have. It can even send the signal that you're an inexperienced speaker who is speaking by the book, without a better idea for how to begin your speech.

Having said all that, however, starting a speech with a joke or humorous story can also still be quite effective. If it works and the audience laughs, they will be entertained and have a positive feeling about you from the start, making them more willing to hear what you have to say next. For certain speeches, it's not only effective but expected that you open with a joke, such as with personal homages like wedding and anniversary toasts.

If you decide to use a joke as your hook, though, it's crucial that the joke be funny and original. Don't tell an ancient joke that everyone's heard repeatedly. For example, no speech should ever start with the words, "A funny thing happened to me on the way here." Everyone's heard that opening line a million times, and if you start in on that routine, many in your audience are certain to shut you out even before you get to the punchline.

The joke, as with all the hooks outlined here, must somehow introduce the topic for your speech. That's why the best jokes to tell are the ones you can tailor to the occasion, event, audience, or topic. If you are creative, you can take a popular joke you've heard and somehow make it fit the occasion at which you are speaking, or even make up your own joke that is tailored to the audience. For example, if you are addressing a convention of computer programmers, you can write a joke involving computer programmers (e.g., "How many computer programmers does it take to change a light bulb?"). However, you must make certain the joke is good-natured and not mean-spirited. You want to amuse your audience, not offend them.

With any joke you tell during your speech, you must be careful that it will not be construed as offensive. Think carefully about this, too, because some people are more sensitive than you might realize. If there's any risk of offending people, you may want to find another joke or use another kind of hook for your speech.

You also should consider your own personality. Some people are more comfortable telling jokes and therefore tell them quite well. A good joke can die if the person telling it seems nervous, uncomfortable, or lacks good comic timing. You probably know if you're a good joke-teller or not. If you aren't, then don't feel compelled to tell a joke. There are many effective hooks listed here, so you have plenty of other effective options.

5. Cite Dramatic Statistical Evidence

As we discussed in the last chapter, certain speeches draw on statistical findings and data to support or illustrate key points. In some instances, citing a statistic can also be an effective opening hook, although it can be difficult to make the statistic interesting to your audience. In general, statistics are problematic to include in a speech because many people have trouble concentrating on numbers and figures. They hear statistics and immediately become bored and shut out the speaker's voice, or simply have trouble picturing what the statistics actually illustrate.

Statistics can, though, be quite effective when they are presented in the right way. That's true of using statistics in the body of the speech, and it's especially true in the opener. You need to do two things. First choose a statistical finding that makes a powerful statement; and second, present it in a dramatic way. Don't just give the numbers, but tell what those numbers *mean*. Make them relevant to the audience.

The following example simply presents a statistic:

> According to information posted on the American Heart Association Web site, more than 950,000 Americans die each year from some form of cardiovascular disease. There are, however, various ways in which individuals might significantly lower the odds of suffering a major cardiac event.

The following example takes that same statistic and makes it more meaningful and relevant to people in the audience:

Fifty people sitting in this room right now are likely to suffer some form of heart disease. That's according to statistics posted on the American Heart Association Web site, which reports that more than one in four Washington residents have some form of cardiovascular disease. And even more distressingly, heart diseases are currently the number one cause of death in America, killing almost as many people as all other diseases combined.

Before you panic, as I felt tempted to do when I read this, let me also say that the bad news comes with some more encouraging findings. The chance of having a heart attack can be reduced by following a particular exercise and diet regiment recommended by cardiologists. Hearing that made me realize that not every situation need be hopeless. There are things we can all do to profoundly influence the quality and even duration of our future years. And that leads me to my topic today: What actions can we take now that will have a positive effect on the future of this company.

6. Pose Thought-Provoking Questions

Questions naturally have the effect of sparking people's attention because they're presented in such a direct fashion to whoever is listening. By definition, questions require that the person or persons to whom they are addressed make some sort of response. It doesn't necessarily have to be a verbal response shared out loud, as in a conversation or interview; when you pose a question, you inevitably get someone thinking about how they would respond, thereby engaging them on an intellectual and personal level. For that reason, posing a question or several questions can be an excellent way to start a speech, and it's also a relatively easy and fast method for writing an opening.

Some questions are more effective than others in getting people involved with your speech. Be wary of questions that limit possible responses, such as fact-based questions testing basic information that have only a few correct answers. Your speech is not a school exam or game show, and you don't want to put the audience in the position of feeling they are being tested. Instead, your questions should be more open-ended; that means asking questions for which there are many possible ways to respond and no easy or obvious answers. These are the questions that intellectually engage your audience, putting them in an inquisitive, highly responsive frame of mind.

The opening question(s), while open-ended, should also of course be something related to your topic. In fact, asking questions at the start of a speech sets up a possible structure for the entire speech. Your audience will assume the speech is going to explore various "answers" or "responses" to those initial questions. If you choose the right questions at the start, the audience will be all the more interested in hearing the rest of your speech as you explore these "answers."

Examples of Poor Questions with Limited Responses
- Which state is the largest one in the United States?
- What is your favorite song?
- How many times have you said to yourself, "I wish I earned more money"?

Examples of Open-Ended Questions for Starting a Speech
- How do we know a good thing when we see it?
- How do you personally define success? In terms of monetary success? Fame? Having an education? Good health? A family? Or is it something deeper, more profound?
- Why do we make the choices we do? What most influences the decisions we make? Our past? Our friends, family and colleagues? Our individual psychology? The specific circumstances in which we find ourselves?

7. Talk a Bit about Yourself and Your Connection to the Speech's Topic
You can get your speech off to a more personalized start by telling a little bit about yourself. As with the other hooks, this personal description should still be strongly connected to the

speech's topic. You might therefore start the speech by describing how you came to be interested in this particular field or subject matter, or by discussing some of your work or previous experience in this area.

You can also describe in candid terms exactly what draws you to this topic. Audiences like to hear from speakers who are passionate about their subject. If a speaker doesn't seem interested in his or her own speech, why should the audience bother to listen? By telling the audience why you are interested in this subject, you give them reason to be interested as well.

By talking about yourself and your interests this way, you also succeed in sharing some of your personality with the audience. That often can help them to respond positively to you. Rather than viewing you as a generic speaker or disembodied voice lecturing to them, they'll respond to you like a fellow human being trying to communicate with them.

Make certain, though, that you avoid sounding cocky or egotistical, which is always a danger when speakers talk about themselves. This is not the time to expound your numerous achievements or recite items from your resume (chances are that someone will introduce you and cover this material anyway). Instead, it is an opportunity, as with some of the other hooks, to tell a dramatic story that will immediately engage the audience's attention and introduce the topic.

There's one particularly effective way to talk about yourself as your hook without any danger of the audience thinking you're egotistical—that is to use some self-deprecating humor. Share an amusing story about yourself in which you reveal yourself not as brilliant or flawless but human. For example, if you are really nervous about speaking, start the speech by saying, "I haven't been this nervous since. . ." and go on to describe a previous nerve-wracking experience.

This kind of self-deprecating remark will usually make the audience smile, and they'll appreciate your honesty. However, if you use self-deprecating humor, it has to come across as sincere, and not like a false display of modesty. For example, you should never pander to the audience by describing your unworthiness, saying something obviously untrue like, "Of course, I'm hardly smart or talented enough to be addressing you today." You also don't want to reveal anything too serious or embarrassing about yourself. There are limits to what an audience wants to know about you. Stick to a funny, short, true anecdote about yourself that will get the audience to identify with you rather than look down on you.

Example of Self-Deprecating Humor as a Hook

I'm really happy to be here today, but I have to admit I'm also a bit nervous. Well, more than a bit. Frankly, the last time I was this nervous, I was a contestant on "Wheel of Fortune." I was so nervous that when I had the chance to buy a vowel, I asked for a "W." I'm not quite that bad today, maybe because there's no new car at stake. Nerves or no nerves, though, I wouldn't have even considered missing the opportunity today to honor my colleague and friend, Alan Lerner.

8. Make a Direct Reference to Your Audience

If most of your audience share something in common—such as the same profession or interests or home town—you might be able to tie this information into your opening. People always like to hear something about themselves, especially a compliment. If you are going to talk about your audience, make certain you have something good to say about them. Don't ever put your audience down, even as a joke.

It's also important that your compliments be sincere and specific. If you are obviously pandering to your audience, praising them without any real reason to, you'll really turn them off, no matter how positive you sound. Take the time to find out more about the audience before the speech, and say something specific about them in the opening. For example, if you want to praise their city or company, learn more about it and find something interesting, unique, and truly worth praising to talk about. They'll appreciate that you took the time to learn more about them.

Example

I understand congratulations are in order. I've been told that this week marks your company's 50th anniversary, which is certainly an occasion worth celebrating. If I had known, I would have brought you all a gift—I think gold is the traditional gift for a 50th—to thank you for all the years of fine service that my family has enjoyed from Connor Home Products, as my parents and grandparents did before us. Well, I might not have brought gold watches or jewelry for you all, but I hope I can provide you with something just as valuable—strategies for improving your services to guarantee that the next 50 years are as prosperous as the first 50 have been.

9. Open with a Striking Visual Image or a Prop

A picture can say a thousand words. It can also be a striking way to start off a speech because it will give your audience something interesting to watch and maybe even surprise them with something unexpected. Most people attending speeches expect to hear a speaker talking; they'll be pleasantly surprised to arrive at a speech and also be given something to look at or watch.

In the last chapter, we discussed the various visual aids and props you might consider using as part of a speech and that, in some cases, you may even have to include in your presentation. However, not all of those materials would be suitable for a hook. The hook has to be a particularly powerful, dramatic, and memorable image. Showing your audience a picture of a pie chart or graph is hardly going to engage them from the start. However, if you show a slide of a dramatic photograph or painting, a film or video clip, you'll immediately capture their attention and spark their interest in hearing what you'll say about this image. Moreover, such visual images tend to be far more memorable than spoken words. They'll stay with your audience long after your speech is completed.

However, you can't just present a visual aid or prop for shock effect and leave it. If you do, people will think you're merely a charlatan with a few clever tricks up your sleeve and nothing substantial to say. As with all the hooks, this opening image should illustrate an important point that relates to your speech.

CONNECTING THE HOOK TO THE MAIN IDEA/THEME

As we've seen with all of these possible hooks, it's crucial that you not only grab the audience's attention but also use the hook to introduce the main idea/theme of your speech. You have to lead your audience from the hook to the main idea/theme and show them exactly why and how they are connected. You can't expect them to figure out the relationship on their own.

You can forge this connection for them by including a transition like the ones in italics in the following sentences:

- *This experience taught me* the value of persistence, which is my main theme today.
- *That story really illustrates* the importance of creative thinking when it comes to dealing with a problem, which is what I want to discuss with you today.
- That joke always reminds that even when things seem to be their darkest, there is always something we can laugh at. *In the same way*, we can always learn something from a failure, something that will benefit us in the future. I'd like to talk today about what lessons we might learn from our recent financial problems that can help us turn things around next quarter.

This connection needs to be made in a smooth, artful manner. You might have to get a bit creative in finding a way to connect the hook to the main idea/theme. Just make certain the connection is smooth and logical; if it is too forced or abrupt, your hook will come across as a gimmick and your audience will be confused or turned off by its irrelevance.

Consider these examples:

> Someone told me that today is actually the anniversary of Kennedy's assassination. I'm sorry that I have to speak on such a sad occasion, but at least my topic is a happy one: our hope for the future.

The preceding example mentions the significance of the date as a hook, but it doesn't go on to make a smooth connection to the rest of the speech. Instead, the hook seems almost tactless in its lack of relevance to the speech. It makes the speaker sound sloppy and unprofessional, like someone who hasn't even thought much about what they will say.

One might, though, with a little thought, make a smoother, more meaningful connection:

> Someone reminded me that today is the anniversary of Kennedy's assassination. All these years later, hearing that brought back to me the pain, shock, and sadness I felt upon hearing the news that day. It also reminded me of how inspired I was by JFK. I remember the famous speech in which he implored, "Ask not what your country can do for you." I've often thought about those words and what they mean. It's a message that still applies today to so much of what we do. In a way, what he was imploring us to do was not to expect change to happen on its own but realize we need to make changes happen. That's a valuable lesson we can consider when it comes to how we conduct our business today.

Unlike the first example, this one finds a way to tie the date to the speech's topic that is logical and meaningful. It also shows how you might combine various types of hooks as a way to introduce the main idea/theme. This speech begins with a reference to the date and goes on to include a quotation and some personal disclosures.

Some hooks are going to be very difficult and perhaps even impossible to connect to your main idea/theme, no matter how hard you try to make the transition. So be careful to choose a hook that you know you can find a way to connect with the main idea/theme.

In addition to writing a transition from the hook to the main idea/theme, you might find you also have to rewrite the main idea/theme itself. In Chapter 2, you wrote down the main idea/theme, but it might now have to be reworded or reworked in order to fit the context of your opening and follow smoothly from the hook. That's fine, as long as you are merely changing the language and not the main idea itself. You shouldn't have to change the speech's main idea—which, as we discussed in the last chapter, should be something important and meaningful you want to share—to suit the opening. The opening's whole purpose is to introduce a main idea that is important to you and to get the audience interested in hearing you discuss it.

THE PREVIEW

The final part of the opening is the preview, in which, having introduced the main idea of your speech, you now briefly outline the more specific points you will discuss in the rest of your speech and identify how you will approach them. Think of the preview as a brief summary of what's to come. This provides the audience with a kind of road map that will help keep them on track as they listen to the rest of the speech. Its primary purpose is to help the audience maintain a clear sense of the speech's overall shape; knowing in advance what issues or topics will be discussed (and in what particular order) gives the audience something to focus on while they listen.

Here are some examples of preview sentences:

- I'm going to tell you about what I did to find and get the job of my dreams, and then share the do's and don'ts of job hunting I learned from my experience.
- There are three main benefits to this approach that I'll discuss: increasing profits, sparking company morale, and decreasing spending.
- First, I'm going to give you some of the history of and background in this field. Then I'm going to share with you some of the exciting innovations being made in it today. And finally, I'm going to explain just how this affects you today.

The preview identifies the way you organize the body and the kind of information you include in it—issues that are discussed in detail in the section on the body that follows. That means you might not be able to write the preview until you've gone ahead and at least planned the body. It's okay, then, to put off working on the preview until later. You might even wait until you've got a rough draft of the whole speech before putting it in. In some ways that's the best approach because then you can be certain the preview accurately describes the shape of your finished speech.

Not all speeches require previews. They're really only necessary in speeches that are longer than five minutes, in which it's important to help the audience get a sense of the speech's overall structure so that they can follow you from one point to another. In a short speech, there's little risk that the audience will become confused or lose the direction of your argument, so it's not necessary to include a preview.

There are also certain speeches whose content and structure is so obvious that the audience doesn't need to hear it articulated in advance. This would be the case with most personal homages, like toasts and award presentations. Everyone knows that those speeches involve telling stories and discussing various achievements of the person being honored, so you don't need to include a preview pointing that out to them.

LENGTH OF THE OPENING

We've just spent a fair amount of time discussing the three parts of an effective opening. When you write the opening, you'll also want to spend some time working on it. It is a crucial part of the speech and therefore requires concentrated effort. Take time to search for and choose a good, appropriate hook. Work on a logical, smooth connection to your main idea. Choose each word of your opening carefully so that every phrase and sentence is sharp and powerful.

You need to spend time writing the opening, but the opening itself must be very short. This is merely the start of your speech in which you *introduce* the main idea/theme. The bulk of your speech should be devoted to your detailed discussion of that idea/theme in the body, so you don't want the opening to take up too much of your total time. More importantly, the audience won't want to hear a lengthy introduction; this only makes them impatient, thinking, "Just get to the point already."

Your opening really only needs to be a few minutes long, even if your entire speech is going to be long. It should never take up more than one-fifth of your total speaking time (so for a thirty minute speech, the introduction should be *no longer* than six minutes). Most introductions really need be no longer than five minutes. (For a short speech, it can even be shorter than one minute.) You should be able to present your hook, main idea/theme, and preview very quickly and then move on to the body of the speech.

THE BODY

After grabbing your audience's attention with a hook that draws them into your speech and introduces your main idea/theme, you now proceed with the body. This is the bulk of your speech in which you discuss the main idea/theme in detail, raise your key points, and introduce any other relevant pieces of information you gathered while conducting research.

As with the three-part format for your entire speech, the body should be carefully ordered so that it is clear, logical, and effective. The body should not randomly bring up points and address them in some chaotic disorderly fashion; this will only serve to confuse the audience, and you'll quickly lose their attention. Instead, it should have a clearly defined order and progression, moving from one idea or point to another, always propelling the speech forward toward its conclusion. Before you begin writing, you should plan the overall shape of the body, thinking about the exact order in which you will introduce your ideas and research.

There are some general considerations to keep in mind about the information you introduce in the body:

1. Relation to the Main Idea/Theme

The more focused a speech is on your main idea/theme, the more your audience will understand it and be impressed by it. On the other hand, if you continually raise topics that are not related to the main idea/theme, your audience will lose sight of its purpose. They won't have a sense of what information is most important or which points you most want to impress upon them. So the first rule about the body is that everything you bring into it must relate to the main idea/theme.

If a piece of information doesn't connect with the main idea/theme, get rid of it. It will only detract from the purpose and power of your speech. Cutting from a speech is easier said than done. Very often, in the process of brainstorming ideas and gathering information, you hit upon some really interesting ideas and pieces of information you would really like to share with your audience. You might find you have to be tough on yourself as you make decisions about what to include and what to edit. Just remind yourself that the important goal is getting your key points and main idea/theme across. Don't worry that the pieces you edit our are lost forever. Good ideas rarely go to waste. You might be able to raise them in a question-and-answer session following your speech, or use them on another occasion or in another speech.

2. Clarity/Logic

The nature of the various ideas and pieces of information you want to raise will often logically indicate a particular order in which they must be discussed in order to be understandable to an audience.

Speeches that obviously call for a logical ordering of points are particularly those that trace chronological histories or establish cause and effect relationships. The most logical way to present a history (such as the history of your company's relationship with a particular client) is in chronological order, beginning with the event furthest back in time and moving on toward the present. If you chose to disrupt chronology and skip around in time, the history would be disorderly, losing the sense of a logical progression.

Similarly, if you are trying to show some kind of cause and effect relationship—such as the causes and effects of declining profits in a company—you must start with the "cause" and then show how it leads to specific "effects." A discussion of an effect with no cause, on the other hand, is like a body without a brain; it's missing the key piece that explains how the whole thing works.

In addition to histories and cause/effect speeches, there are many times when you first have to raise and discuss certain points in order for other points to make any sense. For example, outlining a proposed solution to a problem and then elaborating on the nature of the problem is just plain illogical. A proposed solution is basically meaningless unless you first define and analyze the problem. Similarly, you might find you have to define certain terms or outline basic background information before your audience can follow more complex points.

3. Maximum Impact

In addition to considering the most logical and clearest ways to raise your points and ideas, you also need to think about the kind of impact you want them to have. This is where more strategic planning comes into consideration. You want to present your points in a manner that has the most powerful effect on your audience. Think again about the attorney planning a case for the jury. A smart attorney might save his best evidence for last, knowing that it is the final thing the jury will be exposed to before retiring to reach their verdict and will thereby most remember.

You can also examine your "pieces of evidence" for your speech and make decisions about which order will ensure your speech has the most powerful impact. You'll probably want to start with a strong point, as the beginning moments of a speech are when you are attempting to make a positive first impression on your audience. At the same time, you'll also want to end on your strongest point, as this will be one of the final things they hear from you and will most likely remember.

Examining your pieces of evidence in terms of their strategic value is particularly helpful for those speeches in which some kind of logical ordering is not so apparent. For example, if you are lecturing on a particular subject area or trying to sell your audience on some product or theory, there may not be any chronology to follow. Instead, you'll simply have various individual pieces of information to share. In this case, you have more freedom in deciding the order in which you raise pieces of information, so you may as well make that order work for you. Bring up your ideas and information in a way that maximizes their impact. Start out strong, and end with a big finish.

SPECIFIC CONSIDERATIONS FOR THE BODY BASED ON DIFFERENT KINDS OF SPEECHES

As we've seen, the primary considerations you want to have in mind as you plan how to include information in your speech's body are: relevance to main idea/theme; clarity/logic; and maximum impact. However, there are also more specific factors to consider depending on the type and purpose of your speech. In Chapter 2, we saw the five most common purposes for different speeches. Each of those five types of speeches requires a particular content and structure for the body, is discussed in more detail here.

Storytelling

If the bulk of your speech involves telling some kind of story, you'll usually want to relate it in chronological order. For example, if your speech is the story of how you got your first job, you would logically want to start with a description of the first, meaning earliest, event in that process, such as your first visit to a college career center. From there, you could go on to tell about the next events in the story: preparing a resume, sending out inquiries, going on interviews, grappling with rejections as they came in, etc.

It is possible, though, to disrupt the chronology of a story for strategic purposes. For example, you might want to start a speech by discussing the most interesting or dramatic event as a way of getting the audience's attention, and then going "back" in time to discuss what brought you to that point. For example, you might begin a story about your first job describing your first job interview. You then could return to describing the initial job search that led to that moment, and eventually continue the story past the first job interview in the latter part of your speech.

If you decide to disrupt chronology this way in a speech, it's important that you make it clear to the audience that you are doing so. Tell them how much earlier or later each event is taking place as compared to the previous one. For example, if you begin your speech discussing your first job interview, after describing that moment you could say, "The process that brought me to that nerve-wracking moment began twelve months earlier, when I saw a 'Help Wanted' listing on the wall of the school career office." A statement like that clearly brings the audience from one time to another without any confusion.

If you do choose to narrate events out of order this way, don't skip around too much. You'll wind up having to make too many awkward transitions, and your audience will be needlessly confused. It's fine to do it once or twice for dramatic effect, but no more.

When telling a story, you should also write in a particular style. You want the story to be like a novel, film, or play, filled with lots of vivid detail and colorful description. Memorable stories usually center on dramatic events with some kind of action or conflict; you should try to choose stories that have these kinds of events and make them centerpieces of your speech. For example, in the story of your first job, describing your first interview would be interesting to an audience because it is like a mini-scene in a play, complete with characters, dialogue, and action. You're better off, therefore, in devoting time to telling about that event than some of the more mundane details of a job search (like standing in line at the post office to send off your resumes).

In describing these events, think of them in dramatic terms. Take time to set the scene, describe the people involved, and quote "dialogue." As you tell these stories, use vivid adjectives that clearly convey what took place. For example, consider the following two examples:

- I walked into the office and sat down. Then Mr. Jameson, the Vice President, started our interview. . .
- A receptionist ushered me into the Vice President's Office. It was absolutely enormous, larger, I couldn't help notice, than most of my friends' apartments. It was entirely windowed, and as I came in I had a spectacular view of Manhattan that, combined with my nervousness, made me feel a bit dizzy. I sat in a lush, antique chair that was more comfortable than my bed at home, across from my interviewer, Mr. Jameson, who was sitting behind an oak desk the size of a coffin. . . .

The second version obviously has more descriptive detail. Which speech do you think an audience will be better able to follow? Which story will they be more interested in hearing continue?

Teaching

If the overall purpose of your speech is "teaching," meaning that you are imparting information to your audience about a particular subject, the body will largely consist of presenting relevant facts you discovered while researching the topic and/or sharing your own knowledge of the subject.

Your primary aim for this kind of speech should be striving for clarity. It's not so imperative that you order points strategically, because your aim isn't necessarily trying to convince the audience of something. Instead, you are trying to help them by being as informative as possible. For this kind of speech, then, you'll want to order your points and pieces of information in the clearest, most logical order possible.

These are the speeches in which you would often want to begin with more basic information, such as providing background, history, and definitions of key terms. Once those points are established, you can then slowly build on them, becoming more complex as the audience gains more of an understanding of the topic.

For example, suppose you are invited to teach an office how to use a new software program you've developed. You wouldn't want to begin with something too complex, such as how to format text and graphic design capabilities. You would start with the essentials: turning on the computer, creating a new document, naming and saving a file. After starting with those important basics, you could then get into the more complicated features. Depending on the size of your audience and the length of time you have to speak, you might stop several times during the speech to recap important points and even ask if there are any questions. In so doing, you ensure most of your audience members understand these basic principles before proceeding, keeping most of them following along with you from point to point without getting lost.

It's particularly important when teaching that you are also careful to use terms the audience understands, or take the time to define the ones they don't. If you are familiar with a certain subject, you are also probably very familiar with the terminology related to it. You probably use certain words and phrases all the time without thinking about it. When you go to speak, though, you need to think carefully about your audience and their levels of experience and education. This means you might have to define these terms for them, especially the first time you use them in the speech.

At the same time, you don't want to speak down to your audience, over explaining principles or defining what they already know. That's why you need to have as clear a picture of your audience as possible when you sit down to write. For example, if you go to teach about a new software program, you might consider how much exposure your audience has had to computers. If they've been using a computer for years and you are merely showing them a new program, you don't need to define basic terms like "hard drive," "mouse," and "disk drive." If you did define these terms to that kind of computer-savvy audience, they might even resent it. However, if you are talking to people who've never used a computer in their lives, they would greatly appreciate the explanations.

In a situation in which the audience is more diverse, you can be a more diplomatic moderator. You might, for example, begin the body by saying, "I know some of you know this already, but just to be certain we're all on the same track, I want to go over some of the basic terms and key information before I move on." In that matter, you show those audience members who do have experience that you are aware of their presence. They'll be encouraged to know you plan on getting to more complex material imminently. Similarly, you might tell your audience that if you use a term they do not understand they should feel free to raise their hands. It will be worth being interrupted occasionally if it helps you keep most of your audience involved with your speech.

Selling

If you are giving a speech that involves "selling" something—be it some kind of product or service you or your company provides, or a particular viewpoint or theory you want others to share with you—you should pay particular attention to developing a strategic plan of attack.

With these kinds of speeches, you want to have a powerful impact on the audience, persuading them to "buy" whatever you are talking to them about. Use the most persuasive language you can. That means removing unnecessary qualifiers like "sometimes" or "in certain cases" or "if at all possible." Instead, you want to use strong, crisp, convincing language, including compelling statements like, "It is imperative that" or "Obviously one must conclude."

Be advised, though, that your audience won't automatically buy what you are selling merely because you tell them to. The most persuasive language in the world is not necessarily going to convince people to change their thinking or take some kind of action. You need, in addition to *telling them what* to buy, to *show them why* they should buy it. Think of a "selling" speech as a kind of argument, in which you want to prove to your audience the validity of your viewpoint or beliefs. To prove something, you need to include convincing evidence that is hard to refute. Therefore, everything you bring into the speech should clearly and convincingly support the argument you are making.

For this reason, "selling" speeches should draw heavily on facts you compiled while gathering research. Presenting statistics, data, scientific findings, or quoting from well-known sources lends credence to your views, making it more difficult for someone to argue against you. Whenever introducing this material, though, make certain you clearly show how it supports your point. Don't leave the audience to make that connection on their own; they might not immediately see it.

The order in which you present this evidence will of course have an effect on how the audience responds to it. As discussed earlier, you should start with one of your strongest points or pieces of evidence, and end with *the* strongest one. If you think a point or piece of evidence is weak, you are better off leaving it out entirely than including it.

To further convince people of the validity of your argument, you might want to consider in advance what counter-arguments someone might make and respond to them within your speech. In fact, an effective way to organize a speech is to begin with an observation about a prevailing belief or point of view that you proceed to argue against. You might say, for example, "Many people would argue that X is the important point, but I'm here to tell you that Y is what's crucial. Here's why X is actually not all that important. . . ."

If you introduce these kinds of dissenting views or pieces of evidence, just be sure you can convincingly and persuasively counter them. Also, make certain that the bulk of the speech focuses on your arguments, not on presenting other people's. Your voice should always come through loudest and strongest.

Problem Analysis/Solution

If you are going to analyze a problem and propose a solution, you simply need to organize the body into two parts. Obviously, for logical reasons, the analysis of the problem should always precede its proposed solution.

In a way, this kind of speech is also a kind of argument in which you are "selling" your proposed solution. To effectively sell a solution to a problem, you need first to convince your audience that a problem exists, that a solution is necessary, and that your particular one is the best option. That's why beginning with an analysis of the problem is important. In analyzing the problem, you are actually defining the problem and building a case for why it must be solved. You should therefore not only describe the problem, but illustrate its negative effects. If you can bring in factual evidence, such as statistics, data, studies, graphs, and charts to support these claims, the problem analysis will be even more effective.

After convincing the audience that there is a serious problem in need of a solution, you now need to convince them that your approach is the best one. Again, the more factual evidence you can introduce to support your idea, the more likely you'll convince your audience. Don't just *tell* your audience about the benefits of your proposed solution; find a way to *show* them. You might for example describe other situations where this particular solution (or a similar one) proved effective. You might also quote from various experts who make predictions about how these proposals would definitely lead to certain benefits.

As with speeches that "sell," you might want to mention other points of view here, but only in order to refute them. You can outline a few alternative solutions that have been proposed or are under consideration, but then emphasize why your solution is better.

There are certain occasions for which it won't necessarily be your responsibility to present only one solution. In these cases, you are more a teacher than a seller; you are teaching the audience about how to view the problem and various ways it *might* be countered. You should then take the time to present various pluses and minuses for each proposed solution, so that the audience can decide for themselves which they prefer.

Personal Homage

A personal homage, such as a toast, award presentation, or retirement speech, can be more loosely structured than the other types of speeches. As the focus will clearly be on a particular person (or persons), the audience will be able to see how the various parts of the speech are related. You therefore have the freedom to tell whatever stories or bring in whatever information you like, as long as it is about the person being honored. Don't make the mistake of using the homage as an opportunity to talk about yourself; if you mention yourself, it should only be in terms of your relationship and experiences with the person you are honoring.

Although people in the audience will usually be happy to hear several anecdotes about the person, even if they are not necessarily closely tied together, you can structure these remembrances around a particular theme. For example, you might use the speech's opening to identify a particular quality about the person you admire—such as his or her perseverance or sense of humor—that you illustrate through the various anecdotes and experiences you then relate. These more tightly structured personal homages appear more carefully thought out and professional.

A crucial issue regarding effective personal homages is that they must be *sincere* and *specific*. Don't say anything about someone that you don't honestly feel; it will show through and insult the audience and the honoree. At the same time, if you merely talk about how wonderful the person is without saying anything specific about them, you'll sound like you don't really know them well, as if you use this same speech for every personal homage regardless of the individual. Take the time to write a personal homage that is specifically tailored to this person; include details that specifically characterize this individual, or tell stories only about him or her.

If you are asked to give a speech honoring someone you don't know well, take the time to find out about the individual. Talk to friends, family, and colleagues and use your speech to relate what they had to say about this person.

PLANNING THE BODY/MAKING A ROUGH OUTLINE

In order to plan the body for your speech, you need to re-examine your key points, various ideas, and the information you compiled while researching. Look over and reflect on this material with the intention of deciding what to include or delete, and figure out the best order in which to present whatever you do want to include. These decisions need to be made, as we've seen, by considering these factors:

1. relevance to main idea/theme
2. clarity/logic
3. maximum impact
4. specific aspects related to the type of speech and its purpose

Before you write the first draft of the speech, it is helpful to construct a rough outline in which you list the various ideas, points, and pieces of information you'd like to include in the body in a logical and/or strategic order. This will give you a kind of road map to follow as you write the first draft, making the writing process much easier.

Put your main idea/theme at the top of the outline, and make certain that everything you include in the outline can be clearly connected to it. If not, then cut it.

Next, take your list of key points (that you developed in Chapter 2) and see if there is a particular way you think they should be ordered based on logic, clarity, impact, and the nature of your specific speech. Reorder the list, and leave room underneath each key point for additional information.

If you have conducted research and have gathered various facts and evidence you want to include, examine your notes now and see where various pieces of information might best fit into this scheme. Put pieces of evidence beneath the key points they best illustrate or support. If a piece of information doesn't relate to a key point or your main idea/theme, then toss it.

Finally, re-examine the rough outline and fill in any additional information you'd like to include that relates to the key points and main idea/theme. As you create this rough outline, additional ideas and arguments might occur to you, and you should take this opportunity to note them and include them.

As you create this outline, don't worry about making it very formal. You don't need to include formal sentences or rewrite your research notes. Just jot down phrases that identify the piece of information you plan to discuss. For example, you might simply list "Quote from Shakespeare" or "Results of Study" without actually writing the quote or describing the study at this time. As you write your speech, you can turn to your notes for the more detailed information you need to include.

Once you've completed this process, you'll have a rough outline that you can follow as you write your first draft of your speech. This will only be a rough draft, and you may in fact wind up reordering or cutting material as you revise and polish the speech. But this will give you an initial plan to follow and get you thinking about your speech in strategic terms, rather than as a presentation of random, isolated pieces of information.

THE CLOSING REMARKS

If your audience is going to remember anything from your speech, it's whatever you tell them in the final moments. Your closing remarks should include the strongest, most powerful, most memorable writing of your entire speech. The closing should also be the shortest part of your speech, even shorter than the opening. At this point, your audience has been listening to you discuss this particular topic for awhile; they don't need to hear you repeat everything again in detail. The more concise your closing, the easier it will be for the audience to digest—and remember later on.

The most effective way to close your speech is to split it into two parts: the *review* and your *final thought(s)*.

The Review

The review is similar to the preview that you included in your opening. In the preview, you briefly told your audience what points the body of the speech would proceed to address and/or the order in which they would be discussed; in the review, you now briefly recap the main points you made. This review will fulfill two important functions: a) it will repeat points made in the speech, thereby drawing attention to their importance and encouraging your audience to take notice of and remember them; and b) it will indicate that you are coming to a conclusion, which usually encourages an audience to pay closer attention. The audience will then be primed to hear your final thought(s).

The review should be a brief summary of your key points, not a lengthy repetition of the entire speech. You should be able to do it in a few sentences.

Examples of Reviews

- Thus, our declining profits can clearly be attributed to the three factors I've addressed here: poor morale, lack of advertising, and wasteful spending.
- These, then, were the key strategies I used in my job hunt: researching various career options, using the resources of the career center, writing a terrific resume, and making as

many contacts in the business world as I could. These are the same strategies I now recommend to you.

- What's the bottom line? It all comes down to which is more important to you: saving a few bucks in the short term, or spending a little extra now and getting a whole lot more value in the long term. If all you are looking for in a new computer system is a kind of glorified typewriter, then you might as well consider other companies. But if you want a system that can do everything I've shown you ours can do—accounting, record keeping, graphic design, word processing, payroll—then our system is your best bet.

It's a good idea to precede your review with some kind of statement that tells the audience you are now coming to the end, such as

To sum up . . .
In conclusion . . .
Once again, to recap . . .
We have thus seen . . .
As I've demonstrated . . .
This then clearly shows us . . .
In closing, let me say . . .

As with the preview, not all speeches require a review. They're not necessary in shorter speeches or most personal homages, where the audience will have no trouble remembering points you raised in the body. In any speech, though, you need to make it clear to the audience that you are at your conclusion. If you do not include a review, take one of the concluding statements from above and use it to precede your final thoughts.

YOUR FINAL THOUGHTS

We talked earlier about how important it is to grab the audience's attention with the opening. At the closing, you want to go out with a bang. Just as important as your hook was in drawing your audience into your speech, your final thoughts must send them away with a positive impression. In a way, your final thoughts should be like the sound bites we hear public figures use in press conferences all the time—something that is clever, punchy, easily remembered, and quotable. You want to finish off with a well-written statement that will stay with your audience, one they will be able to remember and quote to others later on.

Many of the techniques discussed above as hooks might make effective final thoughts for your closing. For example, a famous quotation might be well written and particularly memorable. The same rule applies here, though, as it did with the hook: A final thought must clearly relate to the speech's main idea/theme. You can use the review to connect the body of your speech to the final thought.

In addition to using one of the hooks as a final thought, there are a few other powerful and effective options.

Coming Full Circle

If you can find some way to return to an image or element from your opening, you'll provide your speech with closure in an artful manner. Do not, though, merely repeat the opening hook. That would only bore your audience, who will understandably think they've heard it all before. Instead, pick up on something in the opening but discuss it in different terms or, better still, build upon it in a way that draws on everything you have just discussed in the body.

For example, one of the hooks discussed earlier quoted a passage from the play *Six Degrees of Separation*. A final thought that returns to that quotation, but now builds on it further, might look like this:

Yes, we may be separated from everyone on this planet by six degrees, but our common bond—this company—brings all of us much closer. The work of one division affects all the others; the work of one individual also has an impact on us all. There are no degrees of separation here. That is something we must strive to remember each day we come to work.

Call to Action

Many speeches are delivered with the intention not only of engaging the audience's attention while you speak, but inspiring them to do something afterwards. These are particularly the persuasive speeches, such as those that try to "sell" products, services, ideas, or arguments to the audience. In these cases, there's nothing wrong with using your final comments to explicitly state what you hope the audience to now do. If the entire speech has done its job and shown them why they should take these actions, this ending can successfully reinforce that message.

Example

That, then, is the situation we have before us. We have just had our lowest earnings quarter in ten years due to the problems I have shared with you. If you are prone to panic and pessimism, then turn your back. However, if you have any hope for salvaging this company—if all you've invested here means anything at all to you —then you must begin implementing the changes I've outlined immediately.

Ponder the Future

Ending your speech with some kind of reference to the future gets your audience thinking about more long-term implications of your speech. This can be a very effective way to ensure your speech stays with your audience beyond the time you actually speak to them. It can also often provide a quite inspirational ending.

Example

We are thus at a crossroads. Two paths now lie before us. One is a route mired in panic and pessimism that can only spiral downward. The other, the program I've proposed today, is based firmly on fact and reason, and will surely put us on solid footing in the near future. On which path do you think we should take the next step?

In addition to asking the audience to ponder the future, this example also indicates how ending with a powerful, thought-provoking question can also serve as an excellent form for your final line.

Any Powerful, Well-Written Statement

In addition to using one of the devices outlined here, any well-written, powerful statement that expresses what you view as the vital point of your speech will be an effective final thought. Think of yourself as creating a short poem or slogan, easily quoted and remembered by the audience.

Example

Coming to the aid of a colleague in trouble: to better our working environment, this is something we *should* do. But more important, to become more caring human beings, it is something we *must* do.

As this example shows, sometimes the best final thoughts are the ones that clearly come from the heart. Use that last moment to express what is most important to you and your audience will respond to your sincerity.

5

Write Now:
The First Draft, Revising for
Clarity, Refining for Perfection

*Write. Just write. Even when you don't feel
like it.*

—TERRENCE MCNALLY

*The act of writing is either something the writer
dreads or actually likes, and I actually like it.
Even re-writing's fun. You're getting somewhere
whether it seems to move or not.*

—JAMES THURBER

You've now taken the time to brainstorm ideas for your speech,
settle on key points and a main idea/theme, conduct research and
gather information, and think about strategies for your opening,
body, and closing remarks. Guess what? It's now time to sit down
and get writing. But don't worry too much about it. Having done
all that previous work, the writing of the speech will now be much
easier for you. When it comes to writing a speech, half the battle
is finding interesting, meaningful things to say. You've not only
come up with those kinds of original ideas, but you've also been
thinking about the best ways to present them. Now it's all a matter of getting that material down on paper in a coherent form.

Make no mistake about it, though, writing is hard, especially
when you first begin. When you sit down and stare at that blank
sheet of paper or computer screen and prepare to start writing,
you may suddenly feel blocked and nothing comes to mind. Your

might even feel frustrated, intimidated, or anxious. What causes those feelings, and what makes writing so difficult, is the pressure you might be putting on yourself to create a polished, flawless work. It's virtually impossible to achieve perfection on the first try, and endeavoring to do so only adds needless pressure and anxiety to the process.

There are so many things you need to pay attention to when writing: expressing your thoughts and ideas clearly and strategically; using correct grammar; incorporating information from other sources. Beyond that, you're trying to make certain your audience will be able to follow along with your discussion, while using intelligent, sophisticated language to make a strong impression. Addressing these concerns simultaneously is nearly impossible.

The good news is that you don't need to worry about all these factors at once. By working on your speech in several stages, you can concentrate on specific, manageable goals each time you sit down to write. That way, the thought of having to write won't create all that tension and anxiety; you'll feel good knowing that each time you rework the speech, you are making it better and better.

THE FIRST DRAFT: JUST DO IT

Writing the first draft can seem like the hardest part of the writing process. Staring at a blank page or computer screen is intimidating because it makes you all too aware of the need for you to produce something. Once you've got words on the page, though, it becomes easier to work because you now have something to work with.

The goal for your first draft is therefore a simple one: putting all your ideas, key points, and the pieces of information you gathered from your research on the page. Don't worry for now about grammar or style. Don't worry about how clear and coherent the writing is. Don't worry about what kind of effect it will have on your audience. Just write and keep on writing.

If you made a rough outline, as discussed in the last chapter, simply follow along, writing about each item as it comes up on that listing. Start with your opening, including whatever hook or preview you thought about when planning your strategy. Then proceed through the body, going from point to point in whatever order you decided was the most effective. Then put in your review and final thought. Try to do this in one sitting, without stopping. That way you won't risk losing your train of thought.

As you write this first draft, don't worry that by putting something on paper it must become a part of your finished speech. All of this can be changed in later drafts. For example, you may later on decide on another hook or final thought entirely. For now, though, just put something on the page, so you can see how it appears and decide if you want to keep it that way or not.

If you find you hit a block—if you get to a point where you freeze up and simply don't know what to write next—mark the spot with an X and move on to another idea, point, or piece of information. You can always go back later and work on the trouble spot. As the rest of the speech comes together, you may more easily be able to rework this section.

Obviously, this will be a very rough draft—choppy, poorly written, even somewhat incoherent. But that's okay. This is just a draft, and it's for your eyes and ears only. You have nonetheless accomplished something here. You've filled up those blank pages with raw material. Like a diamond in the rough, you can now work with this material, refining and polishing it until it will impress anyone who comes into contact with it. That's something you couldn't possibly do when you were facing that blank page or screen.

REVISING: STRIVING FOR CLARITY

The first draft you wrote for yourself; the second draft is where you begin working to communicate to others. For your ideas to have any kind of impact at all, they must first be clearly presented. In the first reworking of your speech, you should therefore concentrate primarily on communicating your ideas and other pieces of information as clearly as possible. You don't have to worry yet about style; that's something you can work on later, after the basic ideas have been clearly expressed.

Return to your first rough draft, start at the beginning, and rewrite it sentence by sentence. This time, though, imagine yourself talking to your ideal audience member—someone who fits the profile of a typical audience member attending your speech who truly cares about hearing what you have to say. As you rework each part of your speech, work to make it understandable to this person.

As you do this, realize that your ideas already make perfect sense to you because they are your ideas. You've been walking around with them in your head for awhile now, so you have a certain familiarity with them. But now you are sharing them with someone who hasn't thought about these things at all. They need extra help reaching the same level of understanding you did. Don't be afraid to take the time to explain things to them very carefully. It might seem tedious to you, but to someone completely unfamiliar with the subject, it will be helpful.

Don't let your writing be too vague or ambiguous. Spell everything out in meticulous detail. Don't worry that you are over-explaining; chances are, you're not, as you'll see when you read the entire speech later on. If you did needlessly elaborate, you can edit it down in a later draft.

As you did with the first draft, you should rewrite the speech from start to finish. Then, walk away. Give yourself some time off from it to clear your head. If you aren't working on a tight deadline, put it away for at least a day. If you don't have that much time available, take a couple of hours off. Go for a walk or do something else relaxing.

After your break, return to your last draft and reread it with a pen in your hand. (If you're working on a computer, print out a hard copy so you can write on it). As you read through it, imagine you are not the person who wrote it, but someone who has never seen this material before. Try to come up with the questions that someone in your audience would have if they were to hear this speech for the first time. Ask yourself the following:

- What makes perfect sense as it stands on the paper?
- What confuses me? What is still vague or ambiguous? What needs further explanation beyond what is already written here?
- What questions do I still have as I read this material? What would I like to know more about?
- What opinions or key points are not really well supported with evidence?
- Where are there gaps in logic or sudden leaps from one point to another? Where does the speech move from one point to another in a way that is too abrupt and/or doesn't make sense?
- Is the main idea or theme of the speech clear? Does everything in the speech relate to it? Is it clear *how* each piece of information relates to it?
- Is it clear what points are most important to the person who wrote the speech?

As you read along asking yourself these questions, write notes in the margins. Be certain you anticipate any questions a person hearing this speech would have and make a note of them. If a section of the speech is confusing and needs to be clarified, put a question mark in the margin to indicate it needs work.

Now, return once again to the start of your draft and rewrite it again, this time trying to respond to the questions and notes you listed. If there is a point of confusion, work to clarify it. If additional information or explanation is required, put it in.

You can continue this process as many times as you like, each time reading over a new version, asking yourself questions about it, and then rewriting the speech (or sections of it) based on those questions. As you work more, you may find there are specific sections that are fine while others continue to need work; you can then concentrate your revision on those sections.

As you revise and rewrite, don't be afraid to get messy. Edit out material or add material if you think it is necessary. Take entire sections and move them around. Do whatever you feel is necessary to communicate your ideas clearly and comprehensively.

At some point, you should be satisfied that the main ideas, key points, and pieces of information are fully and clearly expressed. Now that the speech is clear, it's time to make it stylish.

INCORPORATING INFORMATION FROM OTHER SOURCES

In Chapter 3, we discussed conducting research to gather information from other sources to integrate into your speech. While you write the body, you'll now be including much of that information, which generally falls into two categories: factual information (from books, articles, statistics, studies, etc.) and quotations/paraphrases of other people's ideas, theories, and arguments. This information, like everything else in the speech, must clearly connect with the main idea/theme. Additionally, you should only introduce information from other sources if it supports or illustrates points you are trying to make. The exception is when you quote or paraphrase someone else's arguments or ideas in order to refute them, thereby reaffirming your own point of view.

The information from other sources you include in a speech must be carefully woven into the body. You can't simply list various facts or quotations and expect your audience to make sense of it all. Like the lawyer who argues his case before a jury, you need to explain how each piece of evidence supports your case. All pieces of outside information must therefore be *presented* and *analyzed*. That means you first *present* whatever fact, quotation, or paraphrase from an outside source you feel is relevant to the point you are trying to make. Once that information is presented, you proceed to *analyze* it, discussing it in detail and explaining exactly how it supports (or possibly counters) your point.

In addition to analyzing a piece of information after you present it, you might occasionally want to precede it with a brief introductory statement that gives it context. This will help you integrate the information more into the body of the speech.

Here is an example of an effective way to bring information from other sources into your speech, framed by a contextual introduction and an analysis:

> <u>There is a great deal of evidence that supports the effectiveness of this computer</u> system. In 1989, Silly Stuff Toys Corporation overhauled its entire system and installed the Office Ware Comp. program. According to an independent consultant hired to analyze the company's dealings, crashes and other computer-related foul ups went down 72 percent. Shipping and billing became forty times faster, and general productivity went up by 65 percent. <u>Those statistics clearly demonstrate the value of converting over to Office Ware Comp.</u>

Do you see how the statistics above are made relevant to the audience through a brief introduction that sets them up and the analysis that follows?

REFINING: POLISHING A SPEECH TO PERFECTION

It's not enough for a speech to communicate ideas clearly. You want the speech to have some kind of impact on the audience. You therefore need to pay attention to *how* you express those ideas. Powerful and effective speeches are well-written ones that have style. The writing should be crisp, sharp, punchy, and have a kind of personality appropriate for the subject matter and that speaks to the audience.

After you've revised the speech several times and are satisfied you have a clear and comprehensive draft, reread and rework it once again, this time paying special attention to the style. Look closely at the individual words and phrases and try to make the writing not only clear but as interesting as possible. If you find you tend to use the same term over and over to describe something, use a thesaurus to vary word choices. Just be certain that the new term fits the context of your speech. Not all synonyms are exactly the same. You shouldn't include a word that you've never heard before. Choose a synonym that you know how to use properly.

As you rewrite, keep your intended audience in mind. Make certain that the writing speaks specifically to them at their level. That might mean you need to simplify or further elaborate certain sections. On the other hand, you might need to make the writing more sophisticated to meet a higher level. You can use the thesaurus to help you cater the writing to a particular level.

The next chapter is devoted to writing style and includes many more tips and techniques for improving the quality of your writing. You can read that chapter and use those techniques to refine your speech. Take the time to polish your speech to perfection.

EDITING: FITTING THE TIME

In Chapter 1, we discussed the importance of knowing how much time you have to give your speech. As you write the speech, you're going to want to edit it so that it fits that time limit.

Writing to fit a specific time is somewhat difficult to do, as each person speaks at a different rate. However, as a very rough estimate you can figure that each typewritten, double-spaced page of text equals about one minute of speaking time. This will give you a general sense of how much to write as you work on your earlier drafts. If you are planning to speak for fifteen minutes, write no more than fifteen pages.

As you get closer to a finalized version, you'll want to check the time more carefully. When the speech is near completion, try timing yourself as you read it out loud. Don't worry about your delivery for now; the next section of the book will help you work on that. For now, just read the speech at a slow, steady pace without stopping. Read at a slower rate than you would normally speak; it might sound strange to you to read slowly, but to an audience trying to digest your ideas, it will seem normal. Time yourself with a stopwatch to get an exact sense of the time (in fact, you might even time yourself a few times and average them together; this will give you a pretty accurate rate at which you read the speech). If you plan to refer to props or audiovisual materials, figure that will add a few minutes to your speech.

If you find you can read the entire speech and stay within a few minutes of the allotted time, you don't have to worry about editing it. No one expects you to stick to the exact time limit, and you can always slightly vary the rate at which you read to fit the time. However, if you are more than a few minutes off the mark, you may need to rework the speech.

Based on how much time it takes you to read the speech, you may find you need to edit it down. Read the speech again and look for places to cut material or rework it in a more concise fashion. For example, if you included an anecdote, you might be able to relate it in fewer sentences, perhaps by cutting some unnecessary description. You might, if necessary, replace an anecdote with some other piece of information that makes the same point more succinctly, such as a famous quotation.

If necessary, you may need to cut an entire section of the speech to meet the time limit. Obviously, start by cutting the weakest piece of evidence, or the least important point. Don't cut the material you feel strongest about.

You might, on the other hand, find yourself needing to add to the speech to fill the designated time. This is generally easier to do. You'll usually be able to find some other piece of information to add or a section to expand upon. It's also less of a problem if your speech falls short by a few minutes. You can use the time to take questions from the floor, or let the next speaker begin earlier.

You can, of course, vary the rate at which you read your speech to fit the time, but only slightly. You need to read slowly enough for the audience to follow you or your entire speech will be incomprehensible to them. You are better off cutting out some material and reading what remains at an understandable rate than refusing to cut it and reading so fast no one can understand any of it.

As you continue to cut from or add to the speech, keep timing yourself. Continue making whatever changes you need to until your reading times comes within a few minutes of your allotted time.

GETTING FEEDBACK

Throughout this writing process, you have been working alone; the goal though, is to communicate to other people. Therefore, when you are finished with the speech, you may want to get feedback from some other people before you deliver it to your intended audience. Select people whom you trust and whose opinions you value; either read your speech out loud to them or give it to them to read themselves. (For now, you are solely concerned about how they respond to what you're written. In the next section, we'll work on the way you deliver the speech.)

After they finish reading or listening to the speech, engage them in conversation about it. Try not to grill them about it, asking specific questions to test them as to what they understood, liked, or agreed with. Just have a chat as you would with any friend. By talking casually with them, you'll get a more candid response. You should be able to get a sense of how they feel about the speech and what they got from it without necessarily putting them on the spot.

If you feel comfortable doing so, ask them for suggestions on what to revise. Don't feel compelled, though, to follow their advice. You can use feedback from others to help clarify your speech, but don't be persuaded to change the ideas. This speech is yours, and should reflect your thinking and point of view. If you find, though, that you get a response from your friend you didn't foresee or intend—such as hostility or anger over it—you may want to rework the speech, as this might very well be the same kind of response you would eventually get from your audience.

FINAL CHECKLIST

Before giving your speech the final stamp of approval, ask yourself these questions:

- Does my speech have a hook that captures my audience's attention and draws them into the rest of the speech?
- Is the main idea/theme of the speech clearly introduced? Is there a preview indicating how this main idea/theme will be discussed?
- Does the body make its points clearly, logically, and effectively? Does it follow the pattern indicated in the preview?
- Are all ideas, points, and pieces of information explained clearly and fully? Will anything confuse the audience unnecessarily?
- Does the speech speak to my audience at their level?
- Does one point lead smoothly, logically, and clearly to the next?
- Do the closing remarks include a review that briefly recaps the main points and alerts the audience that the speech is coming to a finish?
- Are the final thoughts powerful and memorable? Will the audience take away what I want them to take away?
- Will the speech as a whole have the impact I hope it will on the audience?
- Does the speech, when I read it out loud and time it, come within a few minutes of the time allotted?

6

Saying It with Style:
Tips and Techniques for Strong Speechwriting

In matters of grave importance, style, not sincerity, is the vital thing.

—OSCAR WILDE

Once you've drafted and revised your speech to express your ideas clearly, you'll want to work on refining it, making the writing sharper, more interesting, and more powerful. A speech can be like a work of art, such as a poem, painting, or novel, with a style and personality all its own. This chapter outlines various tips and techniques to help you sharpen up your speech and give it some style as well as substance.

VARIETY IS THE SPICE OF A SPEECH

There are many different kinds of writing, and many different ways to introduce and describe ideas and pieces of information. Much of the writing in a speech is plain exposition—a straightforward presentation or explanation of something. If your entire speech is expository, it will become quite monotonous for the audience, who will feel they are being lectured to and become bored by the repetitive style. You can vary from expository explanation in a number of ways that will help spice up the speech. Each time you include a new element, the audience will perk up a bit.

For example, in addition to exposition, you can and often should include analysis and argument, as we discussed in the last chapter. This means that after presenting some piece of information you gathered in your research, you proceed to discuss and analyze it in order to connect it to a larger point. In this manner, the speech won't become a listing of facts and tidbits, but will instead weave that information into a more complex and sophisticated discussion.

In addition to exposition and analysis, the various types of hooks outlined in Chapter 3 also indicate different elements and types of writing you can use to illustrate points in a speech:

- short stories/anecdotes
- quotations
- references to popular films, books, plays
- contemporary references (to news stories, trends)
- jokes and humor
- statistical evidence

Throughout your speech, you can use the above elements much as you did in the opening: to grab your audience's attention but also lead them to some specific point. Just make certain that you don't use one technique repeatedly, which will make the speech monotonous. Combining different elements gives your speech variety and novelty.

USE VIVID LANGUAGE

While writing your speech, it's important to keep in mind that ultimately it will be read out loud. It's much more difficult for the audience to sit and listen to a speaker than it is to read words on the page. People can concentrate much more easily on a visual stimulus like a painting or photograph, or even words on a page, than they can the spoken word. You can, though, help your audience better concentrate during a speech by using very vivid language and highly descriptive words that do paint a kind of picture.

For example, suppose you are an advertiser who is speaking to a new client trying to win their business. You could incorporate into your speech vivid descriptions of some of the advertisements you've created, thereby giving your audience something they can easily picture. The more vivid you can make the descriptions, the better. For example, if you merely say, "The ad had a leopard on a sports car," you're not being terribly descriptive. Instead, you can include more vivid details to give a much sharper, clearer picture of the ad: "In the center of the page, set against a jet-black backdrop was a sleek, cherry-red convertible gleaming in a spotlight. Atop the hood was a leopard, positioned as if ready to leap off and attack, its eyes staring intensely into the camera. . ." There are times when you might even use language that appeals to many senses besides sight, describing tastes, smells, and sensations. These kinds of descriptions will particularly engage an audience's attention.

Of course, you won't always have the opportunity to use this kind of vivid language, and overusing it within one speech can seem coy or tedious. However, if you do have a good reason for including some vivid description it can add an interesting and effective part to your speech that your audience will respond well to.

THE POWER OF REPETITION

If you want someone to remember something, repeat it. When you repeat a phrase or sentence in a speech, the repetition emphasizes its importance to the audience, and they'll pay special attention to it. They'll also be more likely to remember it having heard it more than once.

Example

In considering the economic future of this company, it is imperative that we assess the present. According to a front page article in the *Wall Street Journal*, conditions are ripe for a market crash that will send the corporate world reeling, <u>and it's not even a matter of if the crash will happen, but when. It's not a matter of if the crash will happen, but when.</u> That's a thought that has to give us pause.

By repeating the phrase "It's not a matter of if but when," the above speech emphasizes the significance of that statement. Hearing the phrase twice will certainly get anyone in the audience to take special notice of it.

The above example also indicates the proper way to handle repetition in a speech. You should only repeat something that is worth repeating. If you repeat something that is unimportant, the audience will feel you are talking down to them the way a schoolteacher does to young children. You also don't want to use this technique repeatedly, as it will lose its effectiveness. Save the opportunity to repeat statements for those times when you really want to make a point.

In addition to repeating the same statement in consecutive sentences, you can repeat a statement throughout a speech. You might, for example, introduce a quote or phrase that functions as the theme of your entire speech, and repeat it at significant points throughout the speech. This provides a speech with a powerful unifying element that holds it tightly together.

Example

. . . . As Bob Dylan once sang, "<u>A hard rain's gonna fall</u>." Looking at our present economic situation, that's exactly the position we're currently in.

<u>A hard rain's gonna fall.</u> Open today's *Wall Street Journal*, and you'll find an article in which leading economists claim that it's not a question of if the market will crash but when. . . .

<u>A hard rain's gonna fall.</u> Our main subscriber base is aging, and studies indicate that as they do, they'll have

less need of our products. If we don't find a way to cultivate new consumers in a younger market, within 20 years we can expect a more than 50% decrease in sales. . . .

A hard rain's gonna fall. The costs of materials for our products are increasing at a significantly higher rate than our price increases. Every year it's costing us more money to make our products, and we're selling them for less. That means less and less money in our own pockets at the end of the week. . . .

Assessing the economic situation of our company, it's clear a hard rain is gonna fall for us. The question then is what are we going to do when it starts to rain?

THE NOVELTY OF REPETITION WITH A DIFFERENCE

In addition to repeating statements in and throughout a speech, you can use the technique of "repeating with a difference." This means you repeat a particular statement, but change it slightly in terms of the wording. The repetition invites the audience to pay closer attention, but the variation in wording keeps the speech interesting and enables you to make additional points. This technique can be particularly effective in your closing remarks.

Example

It's time for this company to show its stuff. It's time for all of us to show what we're made of.

Show me the company that was voted number six on Internet Surfer's listing of top internet service providers. Show me the company that raised its customer satisfaction ratings by more than 32 percent. Show me the company that doubled its total sales within a single year.

Show me the company that accomplished all that in the past year, and I'll show you a company that, in the coming year, can do even better. I'll show you a company that can top Internet Surfer's list for 1998. I'll show you a company that can set new records in customer satisfaction and sales. I'll show you a company whose stock will skyrocket. I'll show you a company whose continued prosperity will guarantee your own.

And most of all, I'll show you a company that you'll be proud to be a part of.

WHAT'S IN IT FOR THEM?

If you want your speech to have an impact on the audience, you sometimes need to show them exactly how and why it relates to them. If you merely present information on its own terms without connecting it to the audience's situation and experiences, it will seem removed from them and they'll have little reason to care. However, if you explain how and why this information does affect them, they'll have a more direct stake in hearing what you have to say.

Whenever possible you should try to make what you discuss relevant to the audience. Don't be afraid to include sentences in your speech that begin, "What this means to you is. . . ." Emphasizing the implications of the points you've made during your speech in terms of how they affect the audience can make for a particularly effective closing remark.

Earlier, we discussed the importance of establishing what statistical information means to those in your audience. In addition to statistics, you may find other kinds of information you need to make more accessible or relevant to the audience. For example, if you are talking about another group of people than your audience members, such as employees from another company, you can compare this information to elements of your present audience's own experiences.

Example

At Silly Stuff Toys Inc., all employees of the company agree to a lower salary but receive a small percentage of company stock in exchange. <u>If that same policy were introduced here,</u> your paychecks next week would have to be decreased by about 15 percent.

KEEPING THE AUDIENCE ON TRACK: CONNECTING THE DOTS

As a public speaker, you act in many ways as a tour guide for your audience. You not only share information with them, but take them on a kind of journey, guiding them through the various points, ideas, and pieces of information from your opening to your closing. You want the audience to move smoothly down the path of your speech, going easily from one point to the next, without losing sight of where they are and where they are headed. If you don't take steps to help keep them on that track, you're going to lose them along the way.

This is particularly a danger with public speaking that you won't have with other forms of communication. When you write something, your readers, if confused, can always go back and reread sections to keep themselves oriented and be able to continue following your discussion. When you're speaking, though, there is no going back. You've got to work extra hard to keep your entire audience following along with you.

We talked earlier about the importance of your speech's opening, especially the preview, in laying out exactly where the speech will be headed. As you write the body, you need to include signs that indicate to the audience where they now are within that plan you introduced in the preview. You should also make it clear to them when you are moving from one major section of your speech to another.

For example, if you tell your audience that you will be analyzing a problem and then offering a proposed solution, you should indicate in your speech when you are moving from one to the other:

Having outlined the various factors behind the decline in profits, I'm now going to get to the good news. I'm going to tell you how we can solve this problem and, in fact, start making a profit within a month.

Before making a major shift in your speech, especially in a longer speech, you may also want to briefly summarize what you have just discussed and then move on. For example:

So we can now identify the three main factors behind our declining grosses: wasteful and unnecessary expenditures; inadequate advertising and marketing; and poor employee morale. That was the bad news. The good news is that having identified the problems we can now come up with solutions, and here are the ones I propose.

Another way to keep your audience on track is to continually create lists with "numbered" items. You do this by first telling your audience that you will be touching on a specific number of points; as you get to each point in the speech, you then identify it with a number.

Example

There are <u>three ways</u> in which my company was able to start showing a substantially greater profit:

<u>One,</u> we began a much more expansive and aggressive ad campaign For the past fifty years, we had only been advertising in magazines aimed at the over-fifty crowd. We now began investing in television and radio as well as print media, and we created a new campaign geared at a wider age range.

<u>Two,</u> we trimmed the fat. We hired an outside consulting firm to study our operations and identify the areas in which we simply spent too much money. Their research identified many places to make cuts, and by following it, we were able to stop wasting much of our operating costs.

<u>Three</u>, we took the money we saved from cutting those unnecessary costs and gave it back to our employees. We gave everyone pay increases, and began a commissions program for our sales reps who now got bonuses based on how much product they moved.

This last change had *two* important results: First, it increased our sales, as our reps now had greater incentive to work harder. Second, and perhaps more importantly, it fostered much better morale overall as all employees felt management was now being more appreciative of their efforts.

The above speech tells the audience that three ways they increased profits will be discussed, and then lists those three items by number as they come up in the speech. The last paragraph also shows how within a numbered point, you can go on to create another list of numbered points.

You might choose to structure your entire speech this way. In the preview that follows your opening hook you introduce the number of points you will be addressing; the body then consists solely of your discussion of these points. You would only want to structure a speech this way if it is a relatively short one that lists only a few items. You don't ever want to list more than five points, as this makes the speech seem too repetitive and can tire your audience.

The important thing to remember with this technique is that you must always first introduce the number of points you will address and then follow up on it, announcing each by number as it comes up in the speech. If you don't actually number your points as they come up, you are going to confuse or distract your listeners, who will now have to figure out where one point ends and another begins.

SMOOTH TRANSITIONS

In addition to the strategies discussed above that help your audience move from one major point to another, you can also include various transitional words and phrases throughout the speech to connect sentences, ideas, and smaller points in a more subtle manner. Here are some examples of transitional phrases you might want to incorporate into your speech:

To build on a previous sentence or point: and, also, additionally, furthermore, as a result, consequently, in addition, moreover

To compare a new sentence or point with the preceding one: similarly, in the same manner, in the same vein, likewise, at the same time, by the same token

To contrast a sentence or point with the preceding one: however, but, in contrast, nevertheless, although, yet, on the other hand

To briefly summarize key points up to now: in summary, in short, to sum up, to repeat, therefore, in other words, to put it briefly, simply put, simply stated

ACTIVE VS. PASSIVE CONSTRUCTIONS

One of the easiest ways to punch up your writing style is to change passive sentence constructions into active ones. Passive constructions, which consist of a form of the verb "to be" combined with some other verb, remove the action of the sentence from the present moment as well as from the subject of the sentence. They can make sentences needlessly wordy or awkward and are particularly difficult for listeners to concentrate on during a speech. Sentences with active constructions sound stronger and generally make the writing more powerful and interesting to listen to.

As you refine your speech, circle all times when you use a form of the verb "to be" and try to rewrite the sentence avoiding that construction by using a more active verb.

Passive Constructions
Declining profits <u>were</u> in evidence this quarter.
Problems <u>are</u> often <u>seen</u> in our computer system.

Changed to Active Constructions
This quarter <u>evidenced</u> a sharp decline in profits.
Problems often <u>disrupt</u> our computer system.

You particularly want to avoid the phrases "it is," "it was," "this is," "this was," "that is," "that was," "these are," "these were," "those are," and "those were," especially when they appear at the beginning of sentences, as they establish passive constructions often in an unnecessarily ambiguous or awkward manner.

Passive/Ambiguous Constructions
<u>It was</u> shown that training seminars improve productivity.
<u>It is</u> often necessary to make changes in order to improve.

Changed to Clearer, Active Constructions
<u>The study proved</u> that training seminars improve productivity.
In order to improve, <u>we must initiate</u> immediate changes.

You probably won't be able to change every single passive sentence into an active one, and there are instances where a passive sentence can still communicate something clearly and effectively. But you can avoid overusing passives by changing many of them without too much trouble. You'll see your writing get much stronger as a result.

AVOID AMBIGUOUS PRONOUNS AND DEMONSTRATIVES
Pronouns are words that take the place of nouns, such as "he," "she," "they," "it." They often help sharpen writing by enabling us to avoid repeating long names and nouns that can burden a

paragraph. However, if the reader or listener does not know which noun the pronouns refer to, he or she will only become further confused.

Read over your speech, look for all pronouns, and make certain your audience will know exactly to whom or what they refer. For that information to be clear, the sentence that precedes the pronoun should include the actual noun. If necessary, take out the pronoun and more specifically describe who or what the pronoun name. You are much better off repeating a noun throughout a speech, or using other words to describe the noun, than including ambiguous pronouns.

Example

The executive committee announced to the office staff that computer foul-ups were creating serious declines in productivity and profits. <u>They</u> had to be eliminated.

In the above example, "They" is an ambiguous pronoun. Who or what needs to be eliminated? The office staff? The computer foul-ups? The declining profits?

The sentence can be clarified by replacing "they" with a noun:

The computer foul-ups had to be eliminated.

A similar problem comes from using demonstratives: *that, this, these, those.* When a demonstrative stands on its own, it makes the sentence ambiguous, often without a clear subject. A demonstrative should therefore always be coupled with a noun.

Example

My secretary is always complaining to me about computer foul-ups. <u>This</u> has to be stopped immediately.

In the above example, what needs to be stopped immediately? The secretary's complaints or the computer foul-ups? The sentence can be clarified by including a noun after "this.":

<u>This problem</u> with the computers has to stop immediately.

A WORD ON USING NONOFFENSIVE LANGUAGE

You should always be careful to examine the language you use in your speech to ensure it is not discriminatory or offensive.

There are ethical factors as well as practical considerations involved here. Ethically, one would hope most people have the consideration not to stereotype or demean others in their speech (my personal belief is that no racist, sexist, or homophobic, or otherwise bigoted remark has a place in a speech for any reason).

There are more practical reasons for avoiding this kind of language in a speech. For one thing, while you personally might not be offended by certain words, you have no idea who in your audience will be. Even if you are addressing a small group of people who you feel you know well, you can never be certain how individuals will respond. (Just think about Ted Danson's infamous appearance in blackface at the Friar's Club Roast for Whoopi Goldberg and the stream of negative publicity it sparked).

More importantly, if you make it a habit to stereotype and demean others, even as a joke, it ultimately reflects poorly on you as a speaker. To be a public speaker, you need to conduct yourself with a kind of decorum, even if you are making a humorous speech or light-hearted toast. To use derogatory words will inevitably come off as small-minded and petty.

In addition to blatantly offensive remarks, though, there are many other words that today are considered unnecessarily demeaning or biased. It's therefore worth the time for you to read through your speech and make certain all your language is nondiscriminatory.

The following are the favored terms for describing particular groups of people:

African American or black
Asian (or Chinese, Japanese, Filipino, Thai, etc.
    depending on specific nationality)
Hispanic or Latino
Native American
gay, lesbian, or bisexual

Using nondiscriminatory language goes beyond avoiding derogatory or insulting terms to describe various people. It also involves not identifying or categorizing people according to their gender, origins, religions, or affiliations unless this information is somehow relevant to your discussion.

This particularly applies to issues of gender. Sexist language goes beyond using blatantly derogatory words to describe men and women. Any time you needlessly identify a person by gender, you are discriminating by sex. Words containing "man" and "men" are often used in generic fashion to refer to both men and women. These words should be changed to be non-gender-specific, making them neutral and applicable to both sexes:

Discriminatory:	Change to:
chairman	chairperson
policeman	police officer
workman	worker, laborer, employee
mankind	humankind, people, persons
to man	to operate

Similarly, masculine pronouns (he, him, his) are often used to indicate unnamed persons of either sex. In order to rephrase these sentences in nonsexist terms, you can either change all masculine pronouns to include both sexes (he or she, him or her) or rewrite the sentence using plural pronouns which are non-gender-specific:

Every American must exercise <u>his</u> right to vote.

Change to:
Every American must exercise <u>his or her</u> right to vote.
   or
<u>All Americans</u> must exercise <u>their</u> right to vote.

It is also acceptable to alternate between masculine and feminine pronouns throughout a speech, thereby giving each equal time.

The one important exception: If gender-specific language is part of a quotation you want to include, you should not change the wording. Quotations should remain faithful to the original speaker or writer's wording.

IMITATE THE GREATS

Want more tips on effective speechwriting and ways to write with style? Take time to read speeches by seasoned professionals and learn from them. There are several collections of speeches available in bookstores and libraries. Particularly good ones are *Lend Me Your Ears: Great Speeches in History* (edited by William Safire) and *Graduation Day: The Best of America's Commencement Speeches* (edited by Andrew Albanese and Brandon Trissler).

You can also get in the habit of listening more carefully to other speakers and assessing what you find particularly effective. Identify the way these speakers express themselves and the strategies they use to make their points. What parts of these speeches particularly make an impression on you? Why? Can you adopt a similar technique in your own writing?

Read or listen to the masters, learn from them—and imitate them!

Part II:

Delivering Your Speech

7

Modes of Delivery and Speaking Techniques

> *Suit the action to the word, the word to the action.*
>
> —HAMLET TO THE PLAYERS
> IN WILLIAM SHAKESPEARE'S *HAMLET*

So now you've planned and written an excellent speech. Congratulations. Putting that time and effort into planning and writing the speech means you've got something important to communicate to your audience. However, that's only part of the battle. You've now got to work on your delivery.

Make no mistake about it; public speaking is performing. Your audience, while listening to your words, is also going to be aware of and respond to your voice and physical presence, just as they would actors in a play. Actors might be appearing in a Pulitzer Prize–winning play, but if they perform poorly—for example, failing to project their words and/or appearing too wooden and distanced from their parts—no one in the audience is going to appreciate the writing. Similarly, your *performance* of your speech is vital to how the audience will respond to it—and to you.

The *way* you deliver your speech, as much as your words, can communicate certain qualities to an audience, such as:

- intelligence
- authority
- professionalism
- humor
- confidence
- passion
- sincerity
- solemnity

These are all qualities that can be conveyed through your delivery that will then greatly influence how the audience responds to your speech. If you appear to be disinterested and expressionless, speaking in a monotone, then your audience is certain to consider your speech uninteresting and unimportant. However, if you act like a passionate and sincere speaker, then your audience will respond to your speech with the appropriate seriousness and level of engagement.

This chapter will show you how to perfect your delivery so that you can communicate these qualities and enhance the brilliant speech you've worked so hard to write.

SCRIPT OR NO SCRIPT? CHOOSING A MODE OF DELIVERY

Now that you've written the speech, you need to decide how closely you plan to follow it when you go to deliver it. Will you read it word for word from the page, or depart from your script to speak directly to the audience? There are several modes of delivery, each one with its own advantages and disadvantages:

Reading from a Script

You can choose to type up your finished speech and use it as a script that you read from, word for word, the entire time of your speech. This mode of delivery has various advantages. For one thing, it ensures that, after having worked so hard to plan a speech and polish it to perfection, it is now delivered exactly as you wrote it, with each carefully considered word and turn of phrase kept intact. This can be especially helpful when sharing quotations or complicated statistics that must be reported exactly.

This mode of delivery is particularly useful for more inexperienced public speakers and/or people prone to stage fright. Having a script to follow provides security, cutting down on much of the anxiety involved in public speaking. Essentially, all you are doing is reading something out loud, much as you would a newspaper article you want to share with your family at the breakfast table.

The disadvantage of reading your entire speech from the page is that you appear somewhat distanced from the audience and it is hard to establish any kind of connection with them. It's also more difficult for an audience to concentrate on someone reading to them than it is someone who speaks directly to them, as in a conversation. However, as we'll see in a later section, when reading from a script like this, you can still use eye contact and body language so that you do form some kind of connection with the audience. If you are nervous about giving your speech, there is nothing wrong with choosing to read it all from the page this way.

Memorization

Some speakers take the time to memorize their entire speech. Rather than reading from the page, they recite the speech to the audience from memory.

This mode of delivery has the advantage of enabling you to maintain direct eye contact with the audience from start to finish. But there are many problems with it. For one thing, it can be tremendously difficult and time consuming to memorize a speech exactly and in its entirety, especially if it is a long one. As a result, when reciting it to the audience, you might inadvertently sound like someone who is trying to remember something he or she has forgotten. You might have the tendency, for example, to take long pauses when you forget what comes next and look at the ceiling as you try to remember, then sigh with relief and say "oh yeah" when it comes to you. Even worse, you may find that midway through, you completely forget the rest of the speech, no matter hard you try to remember it.

You would particularly want to avoid this mode of delivery if your speech includes anything that must be reported in exact detail, such as quotations or statistics and data. Memorizing numbers and percentages is particularly difficult; when you don't have them right in front of you, they're all too easy to mix up and report incorrectly.

However, despite these disadvantages, this can be an effective mode of delivery for very short speeches, such as toasts or

introductions, as you'll then be able to address your words directly to the individuals in your audience.

Going Scriptless: Talking Your Way Through

Audiences like speakers who speak directly to them without
reading from the page. This way the speaker is able to maintain
eye contact with individuals in the audience throughout the entire
speech, thereby building rapport and fostering a connection with
them. Additionally, when you're not reading from the page,
you're free to use more facial expressions and gestures to enhance
your words.

The audience, in turn, doesn't feel like they're being lectured
to, but like someone is having a conversation with them during
which he or she is earnestly trying to communicate something.

Aware of these advantages, many speakers decide to direct
their entire speech to the audience without ever looking at the
page. Rather than reading the speech, they try to talk their way
through it.

While this does have the advantage of enabling you to look at
the audience the entire time, it is a difficult and somewhat stress-
ful way to deliver a speech. You've got to continue speaking eloquently and clearly, without stopping to hem and haw and figure
out what to say next. It's too easy in this situation for you to lose
sight of your speech's main idea and instead digress and head off
on tangents. For that reason, this way of speaking lends itself to a
more informal and loosely structured kind of speech. There are
certain instances in which that kind of delivery is appropriate.
This particularly works, for example, if you are an expert in some
area and have been invited to share some of your thoughts on the
topic with the audience.

Generally, you only want to deliver a speech without a script if
you are extremely knowledgeable of the subject and are used to
talking about it without any notes. However, you should still take
some time to plan what you want to say, even if you don't write out
an elaborate script for the entire speech. You don't want to have to
come in and improvise the entire speech from start to finish.

Referring to Notes/Outlines

If you want to speak directly to the audience, you don't necessarily have to deliver the entire speech off the top of your head. You *can* bring some notes with you to keep you focused on the topic and help you stay on track for the entire speech. For example, if you are talking directly to the audience and then suddenly reach a point when you don't know what to say next, you can refer to your notes for a reminder. Similarly, if you want to include quotations and report statistics and data, you can put that information on paper in full and read those sections when you get to that part of your speech. That way you don't need to memorize this information and you won't risk misquoting or reporting the wrong information.

If you want to talk directly to the audience but have notes as a backup, the best option is to make an outline of your speech. You can make a rough outline that briefly lists the various ideas, points, and pieces of information you want to discuss in the order in which you plan to discuss them (as described in Chapter 4). Within that outline, you can also include any quotations or statistics that you want to read verbatim. Then, when you give the speech, you can talk your way through the outline, going from one point to another. If you forget what you want to say next, you can simply refer back to the outline. Make certain to type up a neat version of the outline for easy reading.

Some speakers choose to put this information on index cards. Each card lists one single point or piece of information, and they are then put in the correct order. As you discuss each card, you then remove it and move onto the next. The only problem with this method is that you might have a huge stack of cards, and you run the risk of accidentally mixing up their order. You'd have big problems, for example, if you dropped the cards or if they fell from the lectern. Typing up an outline is probably more efficient; there will be far fewer pages than cards, and you can staple them together.

Script and Scriptless: Combining Delivery Modes

As you can see from the discussion of the modes of delivery above, each has its pluses and minuses. It is possible, though, to have the best of all possible worlds by combining all of these approaches. As we've talked about throughout this book, it's important that speeches be well written so that they communicate ideas clearly and make a strong impression on the audience. Having spent all that time working on writing an effective speech, you should now use what you've written. While speaking directly to the audience has its advantages, you lose the power of having a strategically organized, perfectly polished speech.

However, as we've also seen, there are advantages to speaking directly to the audience, such as maintaining eye contact, establishing a connection, and building rapport with them. But you don't have to speak this way the entire time. Instead, you can read your speech from the page, but stop at various points to look directly at the audience and talk informally about particular points. You can do this with those points that you feel most comfortable discussing off the cuff without the help from notes. For example, if your speech includes anecdotes or brief descriptions, you may be so familiar with these parts of the speech that you don't really need to read them anyway.

It can be especially effective to address your opening hook and final thoughts directly to the audience. As these are such important points of your speech, your direct delivery of them can help you capture the audience's attention and dramatically convey the importance of these ideas.

As you practice reading your speech, try to identify places where you feel you can comfortably depart from the script and address the audience directly. In this way, you'll ultimately have a combination of delivery modes that lets you use your carefully worded speech and still establish rapport with your audience.

PREPARING THE SCRIPT

If you are going to read your speech from the page, in full or in part, you should prepare it a certain way to make reading from it easier.

Always type the speech rather than write it by hand. Reading handwriting is too much of a strain on the eye. Type the speech out using triple spacing and then skip an extra line between paragraphs. If you like, you might use a larger type font (14 rather than 12 point) to make it easier to read.

Some books on public speaking recommend that you type the speech entirely in block letters. That's actually *not* a good idea as it makes it difficult to identify the beginning and ending of sentences, where you'll want to take pauses. Do, however, avoid ending a page in the middle of a sentence or, worse, in the middle of a word. Try to end each page with the end of a sentence. That way, when you need to take a pause to turn the page, it will come at a natural break in the writing rather than in the middle of a word or sentence. This will of course increase the number of pages, but that's okay. No one is going to be counting.

Many books also recommend that you clip the pages together rather than staple them. That makes it less disruptive to the audience when you turn pages, as you can simply move each one quietly aside as you move onto the next. However, you also run the risk of losing pages or having them become mixed up, so you actually are better off stapling the pages together. Yes, you will have to flip them over as you read, but that's not nearly as distracting as one might think. In fact, you can use that moment when you flip the page to look at the audience, thereby guaranteeing you have eye contact several times during the speech even though you are reading from a script.

When preparing this script, it's extremely important that you identify any words that might be difficult to pronounce and write them out phonetically. That means you spell the word out exactly the way sounds, not the way it looks. For example, rather than writing "idyllic," you would write "EYE-DILL-ICK." This is especially important for proper nouns and foreign words, as they can be particularly tricky to pronounce. If you don't know the correct pronunciation yourself, find someone who does and have them sound it out for you and put it into phonetic spelling. You don't necessarily need to use the phonetic spelling you find in the dictionary. Spell the word out in any way that captures the way it sounds when spoken correctly and that is also easy for you to read. Put these phonetically spelled words entirely in capital letters in your script, so that they're easy to spot. This will also serve as a reminder to you to take your time and read these words extra carefully.

If you will be referring to various audiovisual aids during the speech, make certain you note in the script exactly where each one will be introduced. Put a note to yourself in brackets and in capital letters identifying the audiovisual item, such as [SLIDE #2] or [VIDEO CLIP OF CAR COMMERCIAL]. You might want to go over these sections with a highlighter to make them particularly noticeable. That way you won't accidentally overlook them when reading.

In the next section we'll discuss various ways to enhance parts of your speech using your voice and physical gestures. As you practice adding these elements to your speech, you might want to include notes about them on the printed script. These notes can function as stage directions, telling you which words to emphasize, where to take pauses, or when to make gestures. For example, if you decide you want to emphasize a certain word or phrase, underline it on the page or put it in italics. If you know you want to take a pause for dramatic effect, either put in a slash (/) or an ellipsis (. . .). You can also develop your own sign system, or write in your own notes in the margins or between the lines. By writing these notes in by hand, you distinguish them from the speech itself and then don't run the risk of accidentally reading them out loud.

As mentioned above, you may decide that you don't want to read certain parts of the speech, but instead will look directly at the audience and talk your way through these points. As you decide which parts of the speech you will do this for, you should note them on the page. Take a bright colored pen and underline or draw a large bracket alongside any paragraphs you plan to talk your way through. That will make it easy for you to spot when to look up and start talking directly to the audience, as well as where to resume reading after you have finished. Do not, however, cut these sections entirely from the speech. By keeping them in, you give yourself a backup. You might at the last minute find you are uncomfortable taking directly to the audience, or that you begin talking and forget what you are supposed to say. In these instances, you can then refer back to the script.

SPEAKING TECHNIQUES: THE TOOLS OF THE TRADE

If public speaking is like a performance, that means you must think of yourself as an actor. Actors train themselves in the proper way to use the tools of their trade—the voice, eye contact, and body language—to their advantage. To be an effective public speaker, you also need to understand how these tools work and learn how you can best use them to enhance your speech.

THE VOICE

For a public speaker, the voice is the most important tool of the trade. It's like a musical instrument that you must learn to fine-tune and control to make the precise sounds you desire. There are several components to the voice that you should be aware of and practice controlling. Additionally, you'll want to try to vary the way you use your voice throughout your speech. No one wants to listen to a speaker who drones on, sounding like that robotic voice on your answering machine that coldly announces how many messages you have.

Enunciation: Enunciation refers to pronouncing words correctly and precisely. When we have casual conversations with friends, we tend to skip over or cram together certain letters and letter combinations. We also tend to string words together, attaching the final sound of one word to the initial sound in the next word. When you are speaking before an audience, though, you need to enunciate words much more carefully and distinctly.

Practice reading your speech very slowly, pronouncing each and every sound as precisely as possible. Pay special attention to differentiating consonants that can sound the same (such as "b" and "d"; "f" and "s"). Also look for combinations of letters in which you might mistakenly leave a letter out. For example, in the word "crypt," people tend to leave off the final "t" sound and just say "crip." You need to make the extra effort to pronounce both the "p" and that final "t." Similarly, many people leave out parts of contractions (instead of saying "you'll" they mistakenly just say "you"; instead of saying "shouldn't" they say "shunt").

As you work on enunciating your words, use your entire mouth as you would when chewing gum or tasting wine. Before speaking, try a warm up to exercise the mouth muscles. Try making a tight smile and then dropping it several times. Then try opening your mouth wide and closing it several times. This will help you loosen up the mouth muscles.

As you read, feel free to move your lips and tongue, and open your mouth wider than you normally would when speaking. Imagine that you are reading the speech to someone who doesn't understand that much English, or to someone who reads lips.

Enunciating words extra carefully this way might feel a bit strange, but when you deliver a speech in person, you'll actually sound natural to an audience who is trying to hear and understand each word.

Volume: To appreciate or be influenced by your speech, an audience needs to be able to *hear* it. That means you need to work on controlling the volume of your voice. You want your speech to be loud enough for people to hear, but not so loud that you scream and shout.

To practice controlling your voice's volume, imagine your voice is like a stereo system with various levels. Try reading your speech raising the volume level up a few notches from your normal speaking level. You can also work on projecting your voice. This is the tool that actors use to make themselves heard without microphones in large theatre spaces—they direct their voices to a spot in the back of the theatre.

You can practice volume and projection by bringing a friend with you to some large room, preferably the one in which your speech will be delivered. Have your friend stand in the back of the room, and try raising your volume level and directing your words to this person. Ask if your friend can hear you. If not, try turning up the volume another notch. Continue going up a notch until your friend can hear you loud and clear.

Additionally, you can experiment with altering your voice's volume at times for dramatic effect. For example, if you speak a certain word or phrase more loudly, it will certainly get attention. Even whispering a word or phrase can be effective, if done on occasion and for some specific purpose.

Of course, you may have the opportunity to use a microphone. Only use a microphone, though, if you are speaking in a very large space in which your audience could not otherwise hear you. Speaking without a mike is a more personalized way of talking to an audience, closer to direct conversation, and audiences tend to pay closer attention to speakers who don't use mikes.

However, if the room is a large one and you don't want to have to scream or strain your voice, by all means go ahead and use a mike. If you do use one, make certain that you speak at your regular speaking level. Either you or the technician can adjust the volume level of the microphone to ensure your regular speaking voice is clearly heard by all. If you decide to alter your volume for dramatic effect, do it only slightly. When you speak into a mike and raise your voice even a little bit, it will sound substantially louder. You don't want to speak so loudly into the microphone that you deafen your audience.

Speaking Rate: In addition to controlling the volume of your voice, you can also work to control the rate at which you speak or read. Most people speak at a rate of about 150 words per minute. You want to set an overall speaking rate for your speech that is slightly *slower* than that. It's difficult for audience members to concentrate on a speaker talking to them because they don't have the benefit of words on the page to focus upon. They need to pay careful attention to you and work at listening to you. By speaking slowly, you give them a chance to hear and absorb everything you are saying. What will sound painfully slow to you will sound normal to them.

As you read your speech, keep timing yourself to see how many words you are reading per minute. If it's faster than 150 words per minute, slow down and try again.

Although you generally want to maintain a slow and steady reading rate, you can at times alter the rate for dramatic effect and to vary your delivery. For example, if you plan to repeat the same line twice, you can read it the second time more slowly, as in this example:

> If this company hopes to survive, we simply cannot afford to lose our stockholders. We . . . cannot . . . afford . . . to lose . . . our . . . stockholders.

The slower pace of the second sentence not only provides a bit of variety to the reading rhythm, but also draws special attention to the line, giving it more dramatic impact.

Similarly, you might want to speed up at times to build suspense. For example, a speaker could choose to read each succeeding line in the following segment of a speech slightly faster:

> If we lose this account, we'll lose the steady income we depend on to keep things running, with devastating consequences:
> One, we'll have to let forty employees go.
> Two, we'll have to cut out overtime pay and bonuses.

Three, employee morale will sag and productivity will
   drop.
Four, news of the loss will lead stock prices to drop.
Five, we'll lose shareholders.
Six, we'll be wide open for a hostile takeover.
Basically, we'll be finished.

By reading these lines faster and faster, the speaker would communicate the sense of chaos and desperation that would result from the loss of this account.

Of course, if you do decide to speed up part of your speech for dramatic effect, don't do it so quickly that no one can follow you.

Inflection/Tone: When you speak normally with other people, such as when you converse with friends or colleagues, you constantly alternate the tone and inflection of your voice. You do this without even thinking about it. These changes often reflect—and communicate—your feelings about what you are saying. When something makes you feel good, you talk about it in a certain way. When a word or phrase is particularly important, you change the way you say it to stress its importance.

Many speakers, though, make the mistake of removing all inflection and shifts in tone from their speech, instead reading in monotone. Their enunciation, volume, and reading rate might still be perfect, but by making each and every word sound the same, reading the entire speech without variation or emotion, the speaker sounds like a robot devoid of emotion or personality. That kind of delivery can kill a speech. Audience members don't want to hear some voice droning on to them about some topic. They want to hear a human being talking to them about things they feel strongly about.

To be a good speaker, you need not only to *read* the words but *perform* them, the way an actor would. Let your tone of voice and inflection communicate the way you feel about what you are sharing with them. If you find something amusing, let your tone of voice show that. If something is important to you, speak more passionately and emotionally.

To practice using inflection and tone of voice in this manner, try reading your speech out loud, imagining you are having a conversation with a friend. You might even want to invite a friend over and read it to him or her. Try to speak the same way you would when talking to this friend about something casual, like what you did last Saturday night. As you read, listen to yourself and think about what you are saying. These aren't just words; they're concepts about which you have a point of view or opinion. Let some of these emotions come through in your voice.

While you can practice reading your speech this way to become accustomed to giving a speech in a more natural, conversational manner, it's not necessary that you decide on a specific tone or inflection for each word and phrase. In fact, if you do that and force yourself to read the speech each time in the same exact way, it will sound much like bad acting—stiff, overly rehearsed, and downright phony. It's okay for each reading of a speech to be different.

In general, though, you should still work on delivering a speech more "naturally" by letting your inflection and tone shift at various points throughout.

Pauses: It's impossible to read an entire speech from start to finish without pausing. After all, you've got to stop to breathe. Poor speakers, though, go right from one word to the next, taking short gasps of breath whenever they need them, even in the middle of words or in places that disrupt the flow of the speech.

You should train yourself to take pauses after each sentence and at the "natural" breaks within the sentence, such as following independent clauses. These pauses should be slightly longer than they would be in normal conversation, as this will help you maintain a slower reading pace and provide breaks for your audience to absorb what you are saying.

You can take an even longer pause after each paragraph. Take the time here to breathe, swallow, and look out at the audience.

This will help signal that you've just finished one section of the speech, and will also provide a short break for the audience to digest what they've heard so far.

Pauses can also be used for dramatic effect. If you say something you think particularly significant, take a long pause after it before continuing to speak. This will draw more attention to that particular comment, giving the audience time not only to digest it but also to really think about it. Similarly, if you pause *before* a particular statement, you then build suspense and get the audience extremely interested in whatever you will say next:

> The rankings of the most profitable agencies in the city are now in. [PAUSE]. Our company is third.

EYE CONTACT

Establishing eye contact is the fastest, easiest, and most powerful way to connect with someone. When you look into someone's eyes, you focus on them as an individual—and vice versa. When you connect with people in an audience this way, they can't help but be involved with and affected by your speech. You show them that you are an individual—not just some disembodied voice—who has something important to share with them.

If you read your speech staring down at your script the entire time, you'll miss out on the chance for that kind of connection—and force the audience to stare at the top of your head. You need to make certain you look up regularly to make eye contact with people in the audience. When you make contact, you need to look at *individuals* in the audience. It's not enough for you to quickly look up and stare into space or at the clock hanging on the wall. You need to look *up* and look *at* someone. However, you also don't want to look at one individual for too long, or to look only at the same person, as this will make them feel uncomfortable. Instead, try looking around the room, catching various people's attention as you do. When you want to be especially dramatic, take a bit longer to look at several different people in the audience.

Even if you don't have a live audience in front of you, you can practice making eye contact. As you practice reading your speech, try looking up and focusing your attention on different objects in the room, such as a chair, plant, or lamp. Try to look at a different object each time you look up. Practice doing this repeatedly throughout a speech, without losing your place when you go back to reading. This will prepare you for looking up and making eye contact with different people during the real speech.

BODY LANGUAGE

Entire conversations can take place without words. Think about how much flirting has to do with body language as opposed to the spoken word. Or try watching television with the sound turned off; you'll find you can still follow the story merely by watching how people move.

Your body language can also enhance your speech in important ways. You particularly need to be aware of your posture, gestures, and facial expressions.

Posture: When you speak before an audience, it's extremely important that you maintain good posture, as this can greatly affect how they respond to you. That means standing up tall and straight, with your head held up—a position that conveys confidence and professionalism. Keep your arms at your sides or place your hands lightly on the lectern on either side of your script or notes.

Practice reading the speech maintaining this posture and keeping your head held up, only using your eyes to look down at the pages of your speech. If you move your entire head downward to read, the audience will have the rather unappealing sight of the top of your head. You'll appear to be slouching, and your words will go right to the floor, making it hard for the audience to hear you. Keep that straight posture and your head held high.

Gestures: While it's important that you maintain good posture, you don't want to remain completely rigid for the entire speech as if you were a department store mannequin. People naturally move when they speak, and these gestures often convey important information. For example, if you slowly shake your head from side to side, it indicates that you disapprove of or are saddened by what you are saying. If you throw your hands up in the air, you indicate your frustration or disbelief about something.

When delivering a speech, allow yourself to make whatever movements or gestures come naturally to you. However, as with alternating your tone of voice, you don't need to choose specific gestures in advance and force yourself to do them every time you speak. This will appear too posed and phony to the audience.

While it's okay to use gestures, you don't want to fidget nervously during a speech, shaking your arms or legs, shifting your weight from one foot to another, or pacing the room. Stand still behind the lectern, and keep the gestures limited to your head and arms.

You also don't want to make gestures that are overly dramatic. Some books about public speaking talk about the importance of making broad, exaggerated movements so that everyone in your audience can see them; if you do this, though, you'll often look overly theatrical, like a silent movie star. There's no need to exaggerate your gestures. Just speak and move as you would if talking casually to a friend.

The exception is if you are utilizing audiovisual materials, in which you sometimes need to slightly exaggerate your movements to help people focus on the images. For example, if you are pointing to something on a chart, you need to use your entire arm to indicate the area to which their attention should be directed, like your local weatherman does to indicate cold fronts moving in on the weather map. (More about utilizing audiovisual materials is addressed in the next chapter.)

Facial Expressions: This is an element of body language that is particularly powerful but all too often ignored by public speakers, whose faces remain an inhuman mask the entire time they speak. Our faces, as much as our tone of voice, convey how we feel. When we are feeling good about something, we smile. When something disturbs us, we frown. When something puzzles us, we raise an eyebrow.

When reading your speech, allow your face to register various emotions. As with bodily gestures, these should not be choreographed in advance. Don't force your face into a stone-like mask or plaster a silly grin on your face. Keep changing your expression to reflect how you feel about what you are currently discussing.

REHEARSING YOUR DELIVERY

Just as you took time to prepare, write, and revise your speech, it's important that you now rehearse it several times. This is the only way you can become comfortable using these various performance tools you have at your disposal. A well-rehearsed speech looks and sounds more polished. More importantly, the rehearsals will help you feel more confident when you actually deliver the speech.

Try to rehearse several times in conditions similar to those in which you will give the actual speech. For example, if you will stand up while delivering your speech, then practice it standing up You can make a do-it-yourself lectern by piling up some books on top of a table and then placing your speech on top of it. If at all possible, arrange to do a test run of your speech in the actual location some time before the event. Then you'll truly feel comfortable when you go to deliver it.

The first one or two times you rehearse, practice reading the speech from start to finish working solely on pronunciation, enunciation, and maintaining a slow and steady pace. Make certain you know how to say each word and that you are enunciating words crisply and clearly. Try to avoid interrupting yourself by saying "em," "um," or "er," and just read the words on the page. Time yourself to make certain you are reading no faster than 150 words a minute. If not, make the necessary adjustments to your pace.

After you have read through the speech a few times concentrating solely on pronunciation and pace, you can then experiment with adding the additional elements described above: changing your rate, volume, and tone/inflection, and adding dramatic pauses, gestures, eye contact, and facial expressions. Imagine yourself not as delivering a speech but as having a conversation with a friend. Allow your voice and body to do whatever comes naturally. However, if you identify places where you know you want to do something for dramatic effect each time you give the speech—such as taking an extra long pause, or emphasizing a particular word or phrase—then note that on the script.

After practicing several times, you might also find there are sections of the speech you know well enough to relate directly to the audience without reading from the page. Note which sections those are, and then practice the speech several more times combining reading from the page with direct addresses to the audience during which you talk without ever looking down at the script. You should particularly practice delivering your opening and closing directly to the audience.

Some books on public speaking advocate video or taperecording yourself while you practice, or practicing while looking in the mirror. This actually can be more destructive than helpful, making you feel unnecessarily self-conscious. We often feel uncomfortable watching or hearing ourselves on tape, when to others we actually seem perfectly fine because we're only acting and speaking the way we normally do. You might find yourself obsessing over aspects of yourself that you can't and don't really *need* to change, and then feeling more intimidated about speaking in public. Instead, try delivering the speech to a few close friends or family members who can give you feedback. This will help you get used to talking in front of a live audience, and you can then ask them to describe how you looked and/or sounded and possibly offer suggestions for improving your delivery.

Rehearse as many times as you like until you feel confident and ready to go. Don't worry about over-rehearsing. When you get to the actual speech, the presence of a live audience and your own adrenaline will add energy and enthusiasm, no matter how many times you've rehearsed. At the same time, you don't need to get obsessive about it, rehearsing every free minute until the big day. Give yourself time off to relax so that you can be fresh and feeling good for the actual speech.

8

Preparing and Using Audiovisual Materials

Having just the vision's no solution,
Everything depends on execution. The art of making art
Is putting it together.

—STEPHEN SONDHEIM,
SUNDAY IN THE PARK WITH GEORGE

We've all heard the expression that a picture paints a thousand words. It's true that an image can often communicate something far more easily and powerfully than spoken text. That's one reason why many public speakers incorporate various audiovisual materials into their speeches. Audiovisual items can illustrate concepts that are tremendously difficult or just plain tedious to try to explain in words. For example, think about how a bar graph or pie chart can clearly and quickly convey statistical information that would take you several minutes to describe, not to mention bore the audience to death as you recite all those numbers and percentages.

There are varying degrees to which audiovisual elements are actually necessary for certain speeches. Some speeches completely focus on audiovisual elements. For example, if you are giving a lecture about modern art, your entire speech might consist of presenting a series of slides depicting various paintings and then telling the audience about them. Without those slides, you really wouldn't have anything to talk about.

In other speeches, the audiovisual elements are not crucial to the speech but can nevertheless be quite useful in helping to emphasize or illustrate certain concepts or key points. For example, if you are head of an ad agency trying to win over a new client, you might supplement your description of the various kinds of work your firm does by showing examples of advertisements you've created.

There are also speakers who choose to incorporate audiovisual elements even when they're not really important to the speech. For example, they might prepare slides and projections that list key terms and catch phrases from their speeches that they flash on a screen while speaking. It's not really necessary to do that, as the audience will also hear the speaker say these terms. However, these added elements can make for a flashier, more eye-catching presentation.

There are many advantages to including audiovisual elements in your speech:

- Not only can they help illustrate difficult or complex parts of a speech, audiovisual elements are attention-getters that alert audiences to take special notice.
- They also add variety to the speech, providing the audience with something to look at and/or listen to besides the sound of your voice, thereby helping you hold their attention longer.
- As it's easier to keep an image in mind than a chunk of oral text, audiences are more likely to remember audiovisual materials you've shown them long after your speech is over.
- Audiences tend to think that speeches with audiovisual elements are more polished, professional, and important.

There are, however, certain disadvantages to using audiovisual elements. For one thing, they can distract and sometimes even confuse the audience, especially if you present too much material, or if the materials are difficult to see and interpret. The other major problem is that when you use any kind of technical equipment you run the risk of it breaking down. If a lot of a speech is dependent on audiovisual elements and the equipment then breaks down, you might find yourself in hot water, with nothing to say or do to fill the time.

However, if prepared and used properly, audiovisual materials can be quite effective additions to a speech, as this chapter will demonstrate. Don't feel though, that audiovisuals are absolutely necessary. A well-written, well-delivered speech can still be tremendously powerful in its own right.

TYPES OF AUDIOVISUAL MATERIALS

Blackboards

Many people don't think of it in these terms, but writing or drawing on a blackboard is a fast, easy, and inexpensive way to incorporate some visual elements into a speech. It's not nearly as slick or professional as other audiovisual presentations, but it does have its uses in certain circumstances. You'd only want to write on a blackboard when giving a speech in a small room in which everyone in the audience can clearly see it. You'd also need to make certain there is a blackboard in the room you can use. If not, you can arrange to get a whiteboard—an erasable board that you write on in magic marker. Whiteboards have the advantage of being clean, colorful, and portable, and you don't run the risk of scraping them with chalk or your fingernails.

If you are artistically inclined, you might quickly sketch something on the board, or use it to draw charts and graphs. However, they're more typically used for writing down notes. Don't write down a lot of information, as this will take up time, be difficult to read, and make the audience feel like they're back in school. Use it instead to write down a few key words, names, phrases, dates, and statistics, and particularly any terms that will be unfamiliar to the audience until you discuss them in your speech.

Flip Charts

Flip charts are any kinds of charts, diagrams, illustrations, graphs, or other visual images that you prop up on an easel in front of the audience. Usually these charts are printed on paper and then mounted to sturdier cardboard pieces. You then stack up the cards in order on the easel; after discussing the one on top, you simply remove it—either casting it aside or moving it to the back—and go on to talk about whatever chart or image is now displayed. You can also have the charts attached together and connected by rings at the top, so that when you want to go onto the next one, you simply flip it over the top. Some speakers use an enormous pad of blank paper; after talking about the top sheet, they then tear it away or flip it back and move on to the one beneath it.

A tremendous advantage to using flip charts is that they enable you to prepare illustrations in advance—thus allowing you an opportunity to make them of professional quality—and then write on them during the presentation. For example, if you want to present a graph documenting your company's profits month by month, you might have a grid printed in advance *without* the specific information for each month yet included. During the speech, as you report the figures for each month, you could then write the information on the graph with a colored marker. This makes for a more dramatic presentation as you are actively involved in showing the audience something rather than just reporting it.

The disadvantage to using these charts is that they can only be used in smaller rooms in which everyone can clearly see them. If you do use them, write with a bright, thick marker to make it easier for people to read your notes from a distance, and be sure your handwriting is legible.

Overhead Projections

An overhead projector allows you to use transparencies that are then blown up and projected onto a white screen. You can have all kinds of images and information printed directly on the transparencies, such as charts, graphs, cartoons, photographs, diagrams, and sketches; you can also write on them yourself during the speech. As with flip charts, transparencies have the advantage of allowing you to write your own notes onto pre-printed materials. For example, you can have a graph or chart printed in advance on a transparency, and while it's being projected onto the screen, you can then write in data with a colored pen. Unlike writing on a blackboard or using flip charts, the overhead projector allows your handwriting and other visual images to appear large enough for everyone in the room to see them, even from a distance.

Hand-Outs

Rather than presenting images on a chart or screen in front of the audience, you can sometimes put that information right into their hands by distributing photocopied hand-outs. When you then refer to a particular piece of information in your speech, such as a chart, photograph, diagram or graph, you can tell the audience which page in their packet they should examine to find it.

This method has the advantage of allowing each person in the audience to be able to closely examine the material. It's particularly useful if you want to share a great deal of information with people, such as charts listing many statistics and percentages, or long pieces of text. For example, if you plan to discuss a particular passage from a book or article in detail, you could distribute it to the audience and then read it out loud so that everyone can follow along. This method is also useful if you are trying to prove a thesis or win an argument with a skeptical audience, enabling you to place evidence directly into their hands.

There are, however, many disadvantages to distributing hand-outs. It can become quite expensive copying materials for large audiences. These materials can also prove quite distracting. Your audience will be shuffling through and reading the material during your speech, even when you're not referring to it. And even when you are discussing the hand-outs, your audience's eyes will be on their laps instead of directed at you. Use them only when other forms of audiovisual presentation are impractical.

Slides

Slides are one of the most popular audiovisual tools used during speeches. They're inexpensive, easy to use, and quite effective, particularly for showing the audience visual images such as photographs and paintings. You can use them to project various images on a screen and make them large enough for everyone in the room to be able to see them clearly. In addition to photographs and paintings, you can also have words and phrases printed on slides. You might, for example, preface each section of your speech with a subtitle that you project by slide onto the screen. However, people have difficulty reading from slides, so you should confine text to single words or brief phrases. Make certain the lettering is bold enough for people to read from a distance without strain. In general, avoid cluttered images; make certain each slide presents a single image or phrase that is easily seen and identified by the audience.

Whenever showing slides, be sure they're in the correct order and placed properly in the machine. Speakers frequently project slides during a speech only to find they're reversed or upside down or out of order. Then they need to stop and put the slides into the machine again, causing an unnecessary delay and losing the audience's attention. Take the time to check in advance that the slides are placed in the machine properly.

Videotape Clips/Film

While slides, transparencies, and charts present silent, still images, videotaped clips let you show images in action with sound effects and even music, thereby adding a particularly dramatic element to your speech. You might show scenes from a movie, television show, or commercial, or prepare a special tape specifically for your speech. For example, if you are an architect and wanted to show your audience some of your buildings, you could prepare a video tour of them that shows off their exteriors and interiors. Or if you've interviewed people for your speech, you can show clips of them speaking rather than merely quoting them yourself. If you want to create a videotape especially for your speech, consider hiring a professional production team to work on it, as the quality will be far superior.

You're generally better off showing videotapes than films, as films require special projectors and can easily break. With a videotape, you merely need to cue it in advance to the right spot, then pop it into a VCR and press play. You'll want to make certain, though, that everyone will be able to see the television monitor on which the video is being screened, which might not be the case in a larger room. Some locations might have several monitors located around the room, so that everyone will be able to see the videotapes that are played. If not, you can request a video projector that projects the videotape onto a larger screen that everyone can see. If you're giving a speech in a large room and these arrangements can't be made, you probably should not show a videotape. As dramatic as a video clip might be, it's not much use if only a handful of your audience can actually see it.

Audiotapes/Music

When talking about audiovisual elements, people tend to only consider visual images. However, you might sometimes want to incorporate audio tapes into a speech, such as musical selections or radio programs and announcements. For example, if you are interviewing people for your speech, you can tape-record them. Rather than quoting from them during your speech, you can play excerpts from your taped interviews, so that the audience can hear these people speak in their own words. This can add variety and drama to a speech, particularly if these people speak with emotion.

Some speakers also use background music during certain speeches and presentations. This can come across as a bit too slick and showy, so only do it at appropriate venues. For example, at a trade show, you might begin your speech or presentation with a piece of music to capture people's attention and entice them to come over to listen to you. Of if you are showing several slides in succession, you might play music in the background to cover the sound of the projector.

Props

Props, as in the theater, are any physical objects that you hold up to show the audience. Certain speeches particularly require props. For example, if you are lecturing about flowers and plants, you would probably want to bring in actual samples to show people. Props can also serve as symbols to dramatically make a point. For example, if you wanted to convey to an audience the wastefulness of your company's spending habits and expenses, you might have a bucket and, as you announce each unnecessary cost, drop pennies or poker chips in it until the bucket is overflowing.

The problem with props is that they can be hard for people to see, especially in a large room. You might in these cases pass around a prop so that everyone can get a close look, although this can take up time and be distracting.

Multimedia Presentations

A multimedia presentation refers to any presentation that combines several audiovisual elements. In addition to the elements described here, such as slides and video clips, they might include live actors as well as several participants who read and/or demonstrate various materials. Multimedia presentations while unquestionably dramatic and impressive, can be quite elaborate, and therefore difficult and expensive to produce.

However, it's now possible to prepare elaborate multimedia presentations entirely on a computer and then project them on a monitor or screen. Certain computer programs enable you to scan in, reproduce, and even create a variety of images—charts, diagrams, photographs, film clips, slogans—and add music, sound effects, and even animation. For example, rather than projecting the title of your speech on a screen via a slide, you can have it move across the screen with a musical background, like opening credits at the movies. You can put together a single audiovisual presentation that you show in its entirely from beginning to end, or prepare a series of programs that you can show at appropriate times during your speech simply by pushing the right button.

There are a number of software packages on the market that, if you know how to use them, enable you to produce a slick, polished, impressive presentation at minimal expense and fuss (such as Microsoft's PowerPoint and Adobe's Persuasion). If you don't know how to use these programs, there are classes and seminars you can attend to learn them. If you don't want to do it yourself, you can hire a freelance computer consultant or a graphic arts designer familiar with computer presentations.

PREPARING AUDIOVISUAL MATERIALS

To maximize the efficiency and impact of the audiovisual materials you use during a speech, follow these guidelines:

1. Only use materials of professional quality. The more polished your audiovisual materials, the more professional will be the impact of your entire speech. You might save time and money by drawing your own charts and writing in text by hand, but the finished product will appear rougher and more amateurish than a professionally printed, typeset chart. You should therefore do whatever you can to produce materials of the highest possible quality.

There are many computer software applications that can help you produce professional-quality graphic images—including charts, diagrams, slides, transparencies, and multimedia presentations. Go to a computer store and ask someone for advice on which software would best suit your needs. Most of this software is relatively easy to learn how to use; there are also classes and workshops that can provide you with some extra training.

If you aren't comfortable creating your own materials on the computer, then consider hiring professionals. In addition to print and design shops that specialize in helping people create audiovisual materials, there are many freelance artists and designers you can hire. Look in the yellow pages, or ask friends and colleagues for references.

If you do create your own materials without using a computer, put enough effort into them so they at least look like some time and thought went into preparing them. For example, if you are writing information on a chart by hand, do it carefully, with a heavy marker in block letters so that they can be easily read at a distance. Remember, the better your audiovisual materials appear, the better you'll look, and the more successful your speech will be.

2. Maximize visual appeal and visibility. Whenever preparing visual materials, do whatever you can to maximize their appeal to the eye. For example, try to include a variety of colors, even on slides that simply list key words and phrases, or on graphs and pie charts. Keep in mind that the colors you choose can affect emotion and mood; if your topic is serious, stick to more sedate colors such as blue, black, brown, green, and deep purple. Lighter colors can be used for more informal topics.

As much as you want to enhance the visual appeal of these materials, you also need to maximize their visibility. Make certain all images you plan to present to an audience are sharp, clear, and able to be seen at a distance. Don't cram too much onto a single slide, chart, or transparency, making it difficult for an audience to focus on what they should be looking at. And avoid showing cryptic or ambiguous images that need lengthy explanations. You shouldn't have to say, "What you're looking at here is . . . " and then give an entire speech explaining what the image is. The images to a large extent should speak for themselves.

3. Make duplicates of all audiovisual materials. You never know if your materials will get lost or become damaged in transit. Always make several complete sets of audiovisual materials for your speech, and then store them someplace safe and dry, where they won't become damaged. Bring several sets with you to your speech, and keep one set at home, just in case. If you really want to play it safe, give one set of materials to a friend or colleague and also have him or her bring it to your speech. That way if you should forget your own copy, you're still covered.

4. Write cues into your speech. If you are going to present several audiovisual materials to your audience, include cues within your typewritten speech to remind you when and where you will show each item. Put the cue in brackets and capital letters. Make certain that you include some key word or phrase to indicate clearly what the item is. For example, you shouldn't just write [SLIDE] but [SLIDE #2: MONET, WATER LILIES] so you know exactly what image will be used during that part of the speech.

Put each cue in your typewritten script at the *exact point* in your discussion that you plan to introduce that particular audiovisual item to the audience. You'll usually want to show an image first and then explain it the audience, so the cue should appear in your speech before the explanation. However, you might sometimes show an image after an explanation for dramatic effect, in which case the cue should come after the explanation in your speech. By putting the cues in these precise places within the text, they function like stage directions. When reading your speech from the page, you'll know that when you come to a bracketed cue, it's time to show that item before continuing reading.

5. Put all your materials in the proper order and number them. If you are showing several items, such as a series of charts or slides, put them in the proper order and number them. Write the numbers on the actual materials. You can put them somewhere where the audience won't notice them, such as on the back of charts, or on the frames of slides. That way if they should somehow become mixed up, you can quickly and easily put them back in the correct order. The cues in your typewritten speech should also list and correspond with the numbered items.

It's a good idea to make a master list for yourself, listing all of the audiovisual materials you'll be using by number with a brief description of each. This can particularly help with identifying slides. Rather than having to hold them up to the light to see what they are, you can look at the number you've written on them and examine the master list for the detailed descriptions.

6. Arrange to have the right audiovisual equipment. When you're giving a speech in which you plan to include audiovisual materials, it's extremely important that you arrange to have any equipment you'll need, such as easels, slide projectors and screens, cassette players, overhead projectors, and VCRs and television monitors. You need either to bring your own equipment, or make certain it's going to be provided by someone else for you.

If you bring your own equipment, you have the advantage of first being able to learn exactly how to use it and take the time to practice with it before the actual speech. If you don't have your own equipment, you might consider renting or borrowing it from someone several days before the speech so you can become comfortable using it. However, whether it's your own or borrowed equipment, you're going to have to get it to the location yourself, which can be burdensome.

You can instead contact someone organizing the event and request that the equipment be provided for you. Many places where you'll be speaking will already be equipped with various pieces of equipment. If not, the event organizers will usually be able to make arrangements to provide you with what you need. Find out if a technician or someone who knows how to operate the equipment will be there, or if you'll need to do it yourself.

In general, you should always inform someone involved with the event that you plan to incorporate audiovisual elements, even if you are bringing your own equipment, just so there's no surprises. Perhaps they prefer you not show materials and instead just speak. Or the location might not lend itself to these kinds of presentations for some reason. For example, if it's a long, narrow room, the sightlines between the audience and where you'll be standing might be poor. Or there might not be enough outlets to plug in equipment. Or maybe there are no blinds or shades on the windows, and when the sun shines in, no one will be able to see slides or projections. For all you know, the event organizers have decided you'll speak outside on a patio or in a garden where there are no outlets at all and the sun will be shining the entire time. You never know. Let someone know your plans just to be certain it will be okay. In addition to contacting someone organizing the event, you might want to visit the location yourself just to make certain that you'll be able to show visual images without any problem in that particular room.

Try to get equipment that's in prime condition. If possible, get slide projectors and VCRs that have remote controls, so you can advance slides and play the tape yourself. If not, arrange to have a technician or a colleague come with you to work the equipment while you're speaking.

7. Have extra rehearsals. Including audiovisual materials always makes giving a speech a more complicated affair. In addition to speaking, you'll now have several other things to worry about, especially if you are operating the equipment yourself. Because of these extra responsibilities, you need to give yourself more rehearsals than you would were you just speaking.

Rehearse your speech several times all the way through exactly as you will present it during the real thing. If you're going to be showing slides, try to get a slide projector and show the slides just as you would during the real speech. If you've got flip charts, arrange them on an easel and refer to them as you speak. If you plan to write on a blackboard, transparencies, or flip charts, do that during the rehearsals.

Try to rehearse using the same equipment you will be using during the real speech. If it's yours, or you've somehow gotten it in advance, make certain you know how to use everything and are comfortable using it. If necessary, get someone to show you how to work everything. Also try to find out what problems typically come up with that particular equipment and learn what to do to fix them. If equipment is already at the location, or going to be provided for you there, see if you can go there sometime before the actual speech to practice with it. If worse comes to worse, you can get there extra early on the day of your speech to check the equipment and make certain you know how to use it.

In the meantime, you can still rehearse and simulate the presentation as best you can. Rather than screening slides, for example, hold each one up and examine it, and then give the same description or discussion of it you plan to during the real speech.

The more you rehearse using the equipment and audiovisual materials, the more possible bugs you work out of the presentation. You should eventually feel as comfortable working with this equipment and referring to these materials as you are getting dressed in the morning. Keep practicing the speech until you can do it from start to finish without a problem.

If someone else is going to run the equipment for you, try to rehearse at least once with him or her so you can work out how you'll communicate during the speech. For example, if someone is going to be operating a slide projector for you, work out some signal that indicates when you'd like to advance to the next slide.

USING AUDIOVISUAL MATERIALS DURING A SPEECH

1. Before leaving, check your equipment and materials. Then check again. On the day of the actual speech, before leaving for the location, check that you have all of your materials together and that they're in good condition. If you're bringing equipment with you, check to make certain it's all working properly. Then check it all again. Put everything in sturdy carrying cases so they won't become damaged on the way to the speech.

2. Get there early to set up. Get to the speech location extra early to set up. Take out all your audiovisual materials and lay them out so you can clearly find them when you need them. Set up your flip charts on the easel in the correct order. Put slides into slide carousels. Lay out markers for writing on transparencies. Have videotapes cued to the right starting place.

If you've got your own equipment, set it all up and check it again to make certain it's working. (I know you've already checked it at home, but the more times you check it, the less likely there will be a problem. Audiovisual equipment is notoriously temperamental. Play it safe and check again and again.)

If you've requested that equipment be provided for you at the site, getting there early will give you a chance to make certain it's all actually there and to practice using it. If there's a technician there to operate it, make certain you meet him or her to discuss what you'll be doing. Be specific about your instructions, telling the technician exactly what materials you'll be using and how you'll signal when you need to use the equipment. If no technician will be present, then practice yourself with the equipment to make certain it's all working and that you know how to use it. If you need help, find someone—one of the event organizers or someone who works in the building—and ask for it.

3. Give the audience a chance to look. During the speech, whenever you show the audience some visual item, give them time to look at it. Don't immediately begin talking, because they won't be listening to you yet. An audience needs a chance to get a look at whatever the item is and begin trying to make sense of it for themselves. After taking a pause, then you can continue speaking.

4. Talk to the audience, not to the audiovisual materials. As you discuss your audiovisual materials, direct your words and attention to the audience, not to the items. If you talk to the slide or chart or prop, the audience won't be able to hear what you're saying. You've already seen this material, so you don't need to keep looking at it. Keep your attention on the audience. Let them look at the image, while you speak to them. If you are writing on a chart or transparency, write first and then look up and continue talking.

5. Make broad gestures. Sometimes when you're showing an audience audiovisual items, you'll need to gesture toward them. For example, you might want to point out something within a chart or diagram, or need to demonstrate how to use a particular prop. These gestures should always be slightly exaggerated, and broad enough so that an audience can see them from a difference.

Rather than pointing with a finger, use your whole arm in a sweeping motion, like your local TV weatherman does when pointing out a storm front. In addition to gesturing with your hand, you can also use a pointer; a light or laser pointer works particularly well for slides and projections.

6. Be prepared for problems and deal with them. The more times you rehearse, and check the equipment and your materials, the less likely there'll be a problem. But problems do frequently occur with audiovisual presentations, and you need to be ready for them. Have duplicates of all your materials with you so that should something become lost or damaged it can easily be replaced.

Be ready for equipment failures as well. Plan in advance what you'll do should certain pieces of equipment break down. During your rehearsals, pretend a piece of equipment has broken down and try to continue speaking. You can try to describe items you would have shown your audience, or if absolutely necessary, skip over sections of the speech that refer to those items. You should be able to give your speech from start to finish even without the audiovisual materials. You'll find more strategies for dealing with equipment problems in Chapter 11: Grappling with Problems. Just be prepared for these kinds of equipment problems so that should they occur during the speech, you won't panic, but will be able to continue with your speech.

9

The Big Day

Don't Panic.

—The Hitchhiker's
Guide to the Galaxy by Douglas Adams

It's finally here! The big day! You're going to deliver your speech, live and in person. Take that advice from *The Hitchhiker's Guide to the Galaxy* to heart. There's no need for you to panic. You've already put time and effort into writing an effective speech and rehearsing your delivery. That means you're much more prepared than many public speakers, and that advanced preparation will be reflected in the quality and professionalism of your final delivery of the speech.

Although the hard work is already done, you still have a lot to do before, during, and after the speech. This chapter takes you step by step through those responsibilities so you'll know exactly what you need to do on the big day.

LAST-MINUTE PREPARATIONS

1. Confirm the place and time. The day before the speech, call someone associated with the event to verify the place and time, and to confirm that you will be coming to speak. Write the correct information down and bring it with you. That will ensure you go to the right place at the right time; in case you forget the address, you'll have it right there with you.

2. Know exactly where you're going. Make certain you know exactly where the speech is to be delivered. Try to get as specific information as possible; for example, in addition to getting a building address, get the floor and room number. If you don't know where you're going, make certain you get detailed directions from someone reliable. It's a good idea to visit the location at least once before the actual speech. This will confirm that you do in fact know where you're going and allow you to see how much time it will take to get there so you can plan accordingly on the big day. This is particularly important if you are following someone else's directions, as it will provide you with an opportunity to test the directions to make certain they're complete and that you do understand them. This will also save you the stress of worrying about where you're going and possibly getting lost on the day of your speech, when you'll have other things on your mind.

3. Check audiovisual materials and equipment. If you are incorporating audiovisual images, props, and materials into your speech, check to make certain you have everything you need. As suggested previously, put these materials in a sturdy carrying case, such as a large portfolio or heavy briefcase, so they won't become damaged on the trip. If you are bringing your own equipment, check it to make sure it's in working order and that you have everything you need (such as extra batteries or a pointer). If equipment is being set up at the location for you, call ahead to confirm that it will be done.

4. Prepare and bring the final copy of the speech. Prepare your final copy of your speech, neatly typed and including any handwritten stage directions you might have added for yourself. Staple the pages together and make certain that they are numbered, just in case they do somehow become separated. Put this copy in a sturdy, clean folder that you can carry with you up to the podium or lectern. If you are using an outline or referring to your own notes, put those in the folder as well.

Prepare at least one extra copy of the speech to bring with you, but keep it someplace separate from your folder, such as in the coat or jacket you plan to wear. That way if you forget your folder, you'll have another copy somewhere else.

5. Gather other notes and materials. In addition to bringing your speech with you, gather together any other materials you might need to refer to or use, such as notes, books, articles, and extra copies of your speech. It's a good idea, for example, to bring a listing of all the sources you consulted in your research, even if you didn't actually cite them in your speech. During question-and-answer sessions, or in a discussion after your speech, someone may ask you for more detailed information about your sources, and you'll then have that information with you. You might also bring copies of your resume or business card, as someone may be impressed by your speech and want to contact you later on for another speaking engagement or in some other professional capacity.

6. Prepare a brief biography of yourself. You should prepare a brief biography of yourself to give to whoever is going to introduce you. Put your name and professional title at the top of the page, as well as the title of your speech. If your name is difficult to pronounce, spell it out phonetically for the speaker. Then include some description of your background and experience; try to limit this to information that is relevant to your speech. You can include some more personal information—such as where you currently live—as long as it is brief and not too intimate. The biography should not be a listing of your experiences as you find it on a resume. Instead, write it out in sentence format as a description of you, so that the person introducing you can simply read it.

SAMPLE BIOGRAPHY:

Alexander Khreyshev [CRY-SHAVE],
Professor of Drama, New York University

"The Show Must Go On: Fundraising in the Arts"

Alexander Khreyshev [CRY-SHAVE] has been a professor of drama at New York University since 1990. He is also the executive director of Play Time, a not-for-profit off-Broadway theatre troupe, that most recently produced an acclaimed production of Beckett's *Waiting for Godot*. His experiences as a theatre producer and director led to his authoring of *The Theatre Fundraising Handbook*, which has become the fundraising bible for many not-for-profit theatres. As a founder and board member of the arts advocacy organization Art Now, he has been an active voice in the current debate over government funding of the arts. He currently lives in New York City, and has recently begun writing his own play about a small theatre company forced to take drastic measures after being threatened with bankruptcy.

7. Select what to wear. Put some thought into what you will wear during your speech, and have everything selected and cleaned well before the actual date you are to deliver the speech.

As people often comment, clothes make the man or woman. Your appearance will provide your audience with their first impression of you. As you want to appear professional, you should dress professionally, even if people in the audience might be dressed more casually.

For men, that means wearing a suit and tie. For women, that means wearing a suit and blouse. Avoid clothing with busy patterns. Stick to solid colors, and try to avoid any that are jarringly bright, as they can distract the audience. Keep jewelry at a minimum. If your arm is covered in bracelets and rings, every time you move you'll make a jangling sound that will distract the audience's attention, as will the jewelry's glare.

Whatever you wear, make certain it is dry-cleaned and pressed. You might be wearing an expensive suit, but if it's covered in lint and wrinkled, you'll look sloppy, as if you don't really care about this event. Choose your entire outfit and make certain it is cleaned at least a day before your speech. You don't want to wake up on the day of your speech and have to start worrying about what to wear.

While you want your clothes to be neat and clean, you shouldn't necessarily wear something brand new. You want to feel comfortable while speaking, and you'll probably feel better if you wear something familiar. If you do want to buy a new outfit, wear it at least once before you give the speech. That way you can make certain it fits properly and become accustomed to wearing it. This is especially true for shoes. It takes time to break in new shoes, and they can be extremely uncomfortable when they're brand new, especially when you are standing to deliver a speech. Make certain you choose shoes that you know will be comfortable when you're standing up for an extended period of time. They should also be well polished. People notice scuffed shoes and they make a poor impression.

Although you generally want to dress formally when speaking, there are times when you can alter what you wear to suit the occasion. For example, at more casual or social events, you can often dress more informally, perhaps wearing only a jacket and tie or a nice sweater and slacks. Make certain, though, that you know without a doubt that the event will in fact be a casual one. You don't want to arrive at a dinner you assumed was casual to find everyone wearing tuxedos and evening gowns!

Even when you dress more casually, it's still a good idea to dress a bit more formally than the other attendees. For example, if you are attending a dinner at which most people will be wearing slacks and dress shirts or blouses, you might wear a jacket and tie if you are a man, or a dress if you are a woman. Whenever giving a speech for any occasion, you should take the time to select clothes that look sharp and always have them dry-cleaned and pressed. Remember, giving a speech is a performance; people will be looking at you and you'll want to look your best.

8. Take care of yourself. When it comes time to deliver your speech, you'll want to be in prime physical condition. The way you physically feel will come through in your delivery of your speech. If you're feeling tired, sluggish, and sick, it will appear as if you're not all that interested in your speech but would rather be home in bed. On the other hand, if you're awake, alert, and energized, you'll appear enthusiastic about being there and deeply engaged in your topic. You'll also be better able to deal with any problems should they arise, and to think on your feet during a question-and-answer session.

In the days preceding your speech, treat your body well. Get plenty of rest, and eat healthy, well-balanced meals. Avoid spicy foods and alcoholic beverages, as they can upset your stomach. You should also avoid the temptation to be out partying or staying out late the night before your speech, which might be difficult to do when you are attending a conference or convention where everyone is out having fun. Wait to have your fun until after your speech. You don't want to have to deliver a speech feeling exhausted with a killer headache.

The night before your speech, do something you find quiet and relaxing. If you're nervous about your speech, rehearse it one more time but no more. Repeated rehearsals at this point won't really help your delivery all that much, but they will make you feel overly anxious. Take time to gather everything you need to bring with you in one place, and lay out your clothing for the next day. Then do something you enjoy. Go out to eat or to a movie. Get a massage. But get to sleep early so you can get a good night's rest. Stay away from caffeine as it might keep you awake that night. If you're having trouble falling asleep, try drinking some chamomile tea, as this can be quite relaxing.

Before the speech, make certain you eat something. During your speech, you don't want to feel weak and as if you're going to pass out or have to listen to your stomach growling. However, stick to blander foods that won't upset your stomach. Stay away from dairy products, as they can irritate the throat and make it difficult to speak clearly. Instead, drink some hot tea with lemon and honey as this soothes the throat and makes it easier to project your voice.

GIVING THE SPEECH

1. Get there early. If you make it to your speech just in the nick of time and have to begin speaking without even catching your breath, your heart is going to be racing, and you'll feel completely stressed out. You'll feel even more anxious if your speech is about to begin and you're sitting in traffic somewhere or still waiting for your bus or subway. Help keep yourself calmer by leaving extra early to give yourself plenty of time to get to your speech's location even if there's some kind of problem that makes you delayed.

When you get to the location, introduce yourself to someone involved with running the event. They'll show you where to sit and fill you in on any scheduling information you need to know. Try to find whoever will be introducing you and provide him or her with your biography. Make certain they know how to pronounce your name.

You can also take this time to check out the room and make certain that everything you require is there, such as a pitcher of water, audiovisual equipment, or a microphone. If you have requested audiovisual equipment, make certain it's there and that there is a technician present to run it for you. If there is no technician, check the equipment yourself to see that it's functioning properly and that you know how to work it.

2. Act like a professional. Generally you won't give your speech right at the start of the event. It will take time for people to arrive and find their seats, and there may be some introductory remarks, other speakers who go before you, or some other activity, such as a meal or reception. The entire time, though, you should behave as if you are "on stage." Your audience will still be able to observe what you are doing, and your behavior and demeanor will contribute to their initial impression of you before you even speak a word.

Make certain you always act like a professional and conduct yourself with courtesy and decorum. If you meet other people before the event begins, shake hands and treat them warmly and politely. When others are speaking, listen attentively. Don't sit fidgeting, checking your watch, and acting as if you're bored and anxious to give your speech. If you seem unhappy to be there, the audience will hardly care about what you have to say. Maintain a professional demeanor from the time you walk in the door until you exit through it.

3. Walk to the podium or lectern with confidence. After you've been introduced to the audience, walk up to the podium (or wherever else you will physically be standing when delivering your speech) with confidence, maintaining good posture with your head held up. Don't shuffle your feet and look downward. Most importantly, look like you are pleased to be there.

Remember, your audience is watching and making judgments about you, even before you speak. Imagine how an audience will feel about you if you shuffle to the podium looking like a death row inmate on the way to his execution. Even if you are speaking about a serious topic, you don't need to look serious until you actually read the speech. For now, you want to convey the impression that you are enthusiastic about speaking today with this audience.

When you get to the podium or lectern, shake hands with the person who introduced you and quietly thank him or her.

4. Arrange your materials. When you arrive at the podium, or wherever else you will be speaking from, take time to arrange your papers, notes, and any other materials you'll be referring to. Take your speech out of your folder and place it before you. If you have any other props or materials you need to take out and arrange, do it now. Try to do this quickly but also carefully. You don't want to take up too much of the audience's time, but you also don't want the stuff to be piled up on the podium making it hard for you to find what you need when you need it.

In addition to arranging materials on the podium, take your watch off and prop it in front of you. This way you can continually glance at the time without making a big show of it, as you would if you had to look at your wrist or a clock on the wall. Each time you look up at the audience, you can casually note the time on your watch. You can then make certain you're not in danger of falling too short of or running over your time limit. (Should you notice that you're running short or long, you can make necessary adjustments, as discussed in Chapter 11: Grappling with Problems).

5. Adjust the microphone. If you are using a microphone, take the time to adjust it so that it's a few inches away from your mouth. It doesn't need to be very close to your mouth, but it does need to be close enough to pick up your voice. Most microphones only need to be about three to five inches away from your mouth. If the microphone is attached to the lectern in front of you, you merely need to shift the angle of the mike to the right position. If it's on a microphone stand, you first need to adjust the stand to your own height, and then angle the mike itself toward your mouth. Sometimes you might wear a small microphone clipped to your lapel or have to hold the microphone in your hand. In these cases you don't need to make any adjustments.

However, whenever using a microphone, you should test the volume level. Don't do this by saying "testing one, two, three," which will make you sound amateurish. Simply ask if everyone can hear you. If you are speaking in a very large space such as an auditorium, ask the people in the back to raise their hands to indicate they can hear you. Not only will this ensure that everyone can hear you, it will provide you with an opportunity to see if the mike's volume level is too high or too low, or if there is static or feedback. If there is a problem with the level, try to get a technician to fix it.

If you've decided not to use a microphone, but you are speaking in a somewhat large room, you might still want to ask if people in the back can hear you clearly. If some of them complain they can't, raise your voice's volume and project more.

6. Give a brief thank you. It's not necessary to start your speech with an elaborate thank you. Definitely avoid clichéd opening lines like, "Ladies and gentleman, I'm so delighted to be here." Those openings are tediously trite, and most people don't even listen to them. Simply say "thank you" and slightly nod your head in the direction of whoever introduced you.

7. Take a moment. Before beginning the speech, take a moment to pause and look at the audience. This will help you capture everyone's attention. When you first come up to the podium, they might still be shuffling around and whispering. But when you pause and look at them, they'll become quiet and look back at you, waiting for you to begin. You'll actually sense them leaning in and becoming more attentive to your presence, as they anticipate what you'll now say. After this moment of quiet anticipation, you can then begin speaking.

8. Deliver the speech. You've got the floor, and all eyes and ears are on you. To have a particularly powerful and effective delivery, remember to do the following:

- Maintain good posture. Stand up tall with your head held high. Don't shift your weight from foot to foot, or keep your hands in your pocket jangling change. Keep your arms at your side, or place your fingertips lightly in front of you on the lectern.

- Address your opening hook directly to the audience rather than reading it from the page. This will help you make eye contact and forge a connection with the audience right from the start.

- When reading from the page, only move your *eyes* downward, not your entire head.

- Maintain a slow and steady speaking rate. Remember to speak more slowly than you would in normal conversation. Most people unconsciously speed up their speaking rate when addressing a live audience, so you should try to speak even more slowly than you did when practicing. It might sound painfully slow to you, but the slower pace will be helpful to and greatly appreciated by an audience trying hard to listen to and understand your speech. If you do alter your reading rate, do it only occasionally for dramatic effect.

- Enunciate clearly. Make certain each word is pronounced carefully and precisely. Avoid hemming and hawing, saying "em," "er," and "mm." Just speak the words on the page. If you are speaking slowly enough, you won't need to hem and haw while trying to figure out what to say.

- Make eye contact regularly. Whenever you direct comments to the audience, or need to take pauses, such as when you need to turn the pages of your speech, look at individuals in the audience. Don't stare at the wall or sweep your eyes across the room. Look deliberately at several people in the room each time you glance up. But don't stare at any single person for too long.

- Make "natural" gestures. While you are speaking, allow yourself to make whatever movements feel natural to you. Don't, however, do anything that is too exaggerated or choreographed. Limit most movements to your hands, arms, and head.

- Vary tone/intonation. Don't deliver your speech in a monotone. As you practiced in your rehearsal, allow your tone and inflection to change as it would were you having a casual conversation with a friend.

- Register emotion. Don't turn your face into a mask or plaster a grin on your face. Allow your facial expressions to reflect how you feel about whatever you are currently discussing—anger, joy, surprise, amusement, sadness, etc.

- Use audiovisuals properly. Make certain you give the audience time to look at (or listen to) the audiovisual material before talking about it. Address your comments to the audience, not to the prop or image.

AFTER THE SPEECH

1. Finish with a dramatic final thought. Remember to address your final thought directly to the audience.

2. After your final thought, take another dramatic pause. Don't grin or breathe a sigh of relief and run to sit down, thereby signaling that you're relieved the speech is finished. Instead, look seriously at the audience for a moment and hold the pause so that your words can sink in and everyone can reflect on the significance of your key points and ideas.

3. After that pause, give a brief thank you and nod of the head. Don't give a long speech thanking the audience for their attention, or complimenting them for being attentive. No one really listens to those comments and they can come across as insincere. You're better off letting the final comments in your speech be the final words your audience hears from you. Don't undercut their impact by continuing to speak about meaningless pleasantries.

4. Keep acting with professional decorum. Don't sit down, roll your eyes, and say, "That went terribly." Don't ask other people around you how you did. And don't breathe a sigh of relief, saying, "Boy I'm glad that's over." Remember, you're still on view to the audience. If you've made a positive impression with your speech, you don't want to destroy it now by acting like an amateur. Sit and be attentive during the rest of the event.

5. Be prepared for other duties. Just because you are finished with your speech doesn't mean your responsibilities as a public speaker are over. For example, many speeches are followed by a question-and-answer session (which is covered in more detail in Chapter 12: Roleplaying). There also might be a reception during which people will approach you to share their opinions or talk further with you about points raised in your speech. Remember to keep acting with professional decorum, treating people with courtesy and respect. It's all part of the positive impression you're trying to make on those attending this event.

6. Feel good and celebrate. You did it! You gave a speech before a live audience. Do not make yourself crazy afterwards by obsessing over how it went, or worrying about minor problems or disruptions. It's over and done with, and there's nothing you can do to change it. Instead, feel good about yourself and your speech. If you took time to prepare and write a speech that conveyed meaningful ideas, and you delivered the speech clearly to the audience, then something was accomplished. You communicated something important to them, and chances are at least some of them were affected by this.

So give yourself a pat on the back for this achievement.

10

Combating Stage Fright

*How does one kill fear, I wonder? How do you
shoot a spectre through the heart, slash off its
spectral head, take it by the spectral throat?*
— JOSEPH CONRAD, *LORD JIM*

*How much pain have cost us the evils which
have never happened.*
— THOMAS JEFFERSON

If you're like most people, the thought of giving a speech before
a live audience makes you feel terribly anxious. Aware that people will be coming to watch and listen solely to you, you may
feel like you're being held up for scrutiny, like a bug underneath
a magnifying glass. Thinking that people will also be judging
you based on this one performance, you can't help but imagine
the worst—that you'll do something so embarrassing you'll be
ridiculed for decades to come. The result of this anxiety is that
you become practically paralyzed by the thought of having to
give your speech—a classic case of stage fright.

If you're nervous about the thought of public speaking,
you're far from alone. Many people describe public speaking as
one of their greatest fears. Even famous celebrities like Barbra
Streisand have publicly acknowledged having severe stage
fright. But she not only manages to go on and perform, she also
knocks 'em dead, proof positive that stage fright can be successfully combated.

This chapter outlines a number of strategies to help you cope
with—and even overcome—your stage fright.

MAKE THE UNKNOWN KNOWN

One of the things that makes us most terrified is the unknown. Have you ever noticed, for example, how much scarier horror movies are when you don't see the monster? Once it shows itself, no matter how gruesome it might be, it's not nearly as scary as when you had no idea what it looked like and imagined the worst. It's the same with new experiences. Anytime we do something for the first time—like going skiing, flying in an airplane, or riding a rollercoaster—it's going to be somewhat frightening. Once we've done it the first time, though, we usually feel much better about giving it another go round because we now have a clear idea what to expect.

The thought of giving your speech might similarly make you feel anxious because, at least right now, it's an unknown experience. Perhaps you've never spoken in public before, or you haven't spoken about this particular topic or in this particular location. As a result, you have difficulty picturing yourself giving the speech, resulting in a vague, unsettling feeling in the pit of your stomach.

But you can make this unknown experience somewhat more familiar. Go to the location where your speech is to be delivered and see it in person. Hang out for a bit and try to make yourself feel comfortable there. Try delivering part of your speech out loud. Stand at the podium or lectern and get a feel for what it's like to deliver a speech in that room. Bring a few friends so you can also become more familiar with the experience of delivering a speech to other people.

Now when you picture yourself giving the speech, you won't feel quite as nervous because it won't be entirely unknown. You'll now be able to form a more concrete image in mind, seeing yourself in a familiar location doing something you've already done there.

REMEMBER: THE HARD PART'S OVER ALREADY

What causes many people's stage fright isn't so much lack of experience (although it is true that the more times you speak in public the more comfortable you'll become doing it) but lack of preparation. For example, many actors report suffering from a recurring nightmare in which they're suddenly on the stage not knowing what it is they're supposed to do or what their lines are.

That's truly a situation worthy of anxiety, but fortunately that's not the situation you're currently in. You *have* prepared. You've taken the time to plan and write a great speech, so you do have something to say. You've also worked on rehearsing your speech, so you know exactly what you need to do when you appear before your audience.

This preparation should help alleviate some of the stage fright you might feel. You do, though, have to remind yourself about it every so often. Anytime you find yourself feeling anxious about giving the speech, say to yourself, "It's okay. I'm ready for this. I've already done the tough stuff. I've got my speech written, and all I have to do is go and read it. I know exactly what I'm going to say and do."

PUT THINGS IN PERSPECTIVE

Something that particularly fosters stage fright is a tendency to have an overactive imagination. Thinking about your speech, you imagine all kinds of things that might go wrong, from the mundane to the nightmarish—you'll flub your lines, get sick, sweat profusely, trip on the way to the podium and be laughed at for years to come. The more you imagine what might go wrong, the more certain you'll become that something *will* go wrong, making you feel more anxious than ever.

If you're prone to imagining things like this, you don't necessarily need to force yourself to stop. In fact, trying to repress these fears can actually make your feel worse; rather than letting yourself think about and deal with these fears, they'll be sublimated into more paralyzing psychological and physical symptoms, like nightmares and stomachaches.

So go ahead; give your imagination free rein. Think about everything that could possibly go wrong. However, don't stop there. After thinking about these things, ask yourself, if some of these things did occur, what would the consequences be? You'll see in Chapter 11: Grappling with Problems that many of these problems can actually be dealt with pretty easily.

But let's say for the sake of argument that something embarrassing happens that can't possibly be prevented or resolved. For example, what would happen if you fell off the podium, or if you tripped and landed smack on your face when going up to give your speech? That would be a pretty embarrassing thing to occur during a speech, and once it did, there would be little you could do about it. What, though, would the consequences be? Well, people might laugh at you. So what? Would that really be so horrible? After, all, it's funny when someone takes a flop, and we've all laughed before when we've seen someone else do it. But at the same time, just because people might laugh, it doesn't mean that they would think any less of you or that your credibility as a speaker would be undermined. We're all human and human beings make mistakes. Most people in the audience would be entirely understanding of that, even if they did laugh. They wouldn't really see your flop as a serious reflection of your intelligence. And if they did, that's their problem, not yours. So, in the meantime, rather than getting upset, you could simply laugh at yourself along with everyone. People in the audience might even admire you more because you dealt so maturely with such an embarrassing situation.

So falling flat on your face, when you think about it, wouldn't actually be all that horrible. Work to put your fears in perspective. If the worst thing possible happened, would it really be so terrible? Remember, this is just a speech. It's not brain surgery, in which a slip-up on your part could cost someone their life. And it's not some daredevil stunt where a slip-up could cost you your own life. No matter what happens, you're not going to die! It may sound funny even to discuss public speaking in these life and death terms. Good. You're better off being amused by your anxieties and fears than paralyzed by them. So every time you feel yourself getting nervous, think to yourself, "I'm not going to die! Get a grip. It's no big deal."

You also might feel better reminding yourself that this experience will come to an end, for better or worse. It's not going to be some kind of sadistic torture that lasts for eternity. No matter what happens, it will at some point be over and done with. For example, if you're feeling especially anxious right before your speech, look at your watch and say, "For better or worse, an hour from now, it'll all be over, and I'll be home relaxing."

ACT LIKE A PRO

If you're feeling like a nervous wreck about having to give your speech, no one else needs to know it. Act like you're completely confident about going to give this speech. Even if you've never spoken in public before, pretend you're a seasoned pro who has done this all the time and doesn't give it a second thought. If people ask if you're nervous, tell them, "No, not at all. Piece of cake."

The reason for acting this way isn't so much to fool others into thinking you're not nervous; rather it's because *acting* like you're not nervous will actually help you begin to *feel* like you're not nervous. Various studies have proven there is a firm connection between our actions and our feelings. We normally think of our feelings as influencing our actions. For example, we know that we laugh or smile when we're feeling good, and frown and sob when we're sad. But it does work in reverse as well. If you're unhappy but force yourself to keep smiling over and over, you'll actually start to feel happy and may even start laughing. So if you *act* like you're a confident, experienced speaker, you'll eventually start to feel more like one.

THE POWER OF POSITIVE THINKING

Just as there is a connection between our emotions and actions, there is also a connection between feeling and thinking. When we have negative thoughts about something, we then start to feel down and depressed. However, you can train yourself to think more positively and then you'll also find yourself feeling better.

Your fear of public speaking probably centers on negative thoughts you have about it, such as:

- I've never done this before and I have no idea what I'm doing.
- I'm certain I'm going to mess something up.
- I'm a terrible speaker. They're going to hate me.
- I don't know why I was invited to speak.
- Who cares what I have to say anyway?
- I'm dreading having to go and talk to these people.

Any time you find yourself thinking negative thoughts like these, replace them with more positive ones, such as:

- I've written an excellent speech that's filled with interesting information and important ideas.
- When people hear what I have to say they're going to be very interested and impressed by it.
- This is an excellent opportunity for me to talk about something that really interests me. I'm looking forward to sharing my ideas and views with others.
- It's so flattering that I was asked to give this speech.
- I wonder who'll be in the audience. It's going to be fun to meet and talk with new people.
- I'm really looking forward to giving this speech.

The more you tell yourself these things, the more you'll start to believe them yourself and feel better.

POSITIVE VISUALIZATIONS

You can couple these positive thoughts with positive visualizations. This is a technique professional athletes use; before they are to do some difficult task, such as trying for a field goal or foul shot, they *picture* themselves doing it. That positive picture gives them a boost of confidence and energy that cuts down the pressure and anxiety. If you can picture it, then you can do it.

You can use this technique as you prepare for your speech. Instead of picturing yourself making mistakes and being embarrassed, picture yourself delivering the speech without a hitch. Better than that, picture yourself giving a speech that blows your audience away. Picture yourself delivering your final comments and then being met with thunderous applause. Picture people coming up to compliment you on a job well done and wanting to talk with you further about your speech. Think about how good you'll feel having given this great speech. When you have these positive mental pictures, combined with positive thoughts, you'll find you're not dreading the occasion so much any more but starting to look forward to it.

RELAXATION EXERCISES

Stress and anxiety can come with a variety of physical symptoms—faster pulse rate and higher blood pressure; sweating profusely; shallow breathing; a variety of aches and pains—that then make us feel more anxious. Relaxation exercises can alleviate many of these symptoms and generally help you feel calmer.

If you're particularly prone to nervousness and anxiety, you might consider taking a yoga class on a regular basis, as this will teach you techniques for combating stress, lowering your pulse rate, and generally feeling calmer.

There are also meditations and relaxation exercises you can do in your own at home, such as this one:

> Sit in a chair with a firm back and place your palms
> face up on the back of your knees. Close your eyes,
> and take several deep breaths. Concentrate for a few

moments only on your breathing. Breathe in and out slowly and deeply. Listen to and be aware of the sensation of the air going into and out of your lungs.

Start to picture yourself someplace you've been where you've felt safe, relaxed, and happy. Put yourself back in that exact spot. Use all your senses, remembering the sights, smells, sounds, and other sensations of being there. Think about this scene for several moments, continuing to breathe deeply. Enjoy the feeling of peace and serenity you have while you are there. At the same time, know that you can always return to this place whenever you need to. Sit for as long as you like here. When you are ready to leave, count slowly to ten and then open your eyes.

If you get in the habit of doing this exercise every day, or whenever you're feeling particularly anxious, you'll find you generally begin to feel calmer and more relaxed. You'll also find that as you become accustomed to doing this, you become relaxed much faster. The first few times you do this exercise, you might not feel relaxed at all. Soon, though, you'll find you begin to feel better towards the end of the exercise. In time, merely closing your eyes, breathing deeply, and quickly picturing that safe spot will instantly make you feel good.

That's a useful tool you can use to combat stage fright. If you're about to give your speech and feeling very anxious, you merely need to close your eyes for a few seconds, breathe deeply, picture this safe scene, and you'll feel calm and ready to go speak.

In addition to meditations like this one, you can do physical exercises to feel more relaxed. For example, you can sit in a chair with your eyes closed and roll your head slowly from one side to the other several times, followed by several complete head rolls all the way around. This will loosen up your neck muscles. You can also do exercises to loosen your mouth muscles, such as bringing your lips back into a smile position and then releasing it several times, and then opening and closing your mouth repeatedly. You can also try chanting the vowel sounds—ah, ay, ee, oh, oo—over and over, really stretching out your lips and moving your mouth as you do. These are techniques actors do to warm up before going on stage, and you'll find they work well to loosen you up and make you feel better about your performance of your speech.

In addition to these relaxation exercises and techniques, do whatever makes you feel calm, comfortable, and happy—get a massage, go to a sauna, sit listening to music—whenever you're feeling nervous. Think of your stage fright as an enemy that must be battled with whatever weapons you have at your disposal. Then encourage yourself to use all those weapons. Whatever it takes, you'll beat that stage fright into submission!

FRIENDLY FACES

One of the things that contributes to a fear of speaking before an audience is the erroneous impression that they're going to be hostile strangers who are anxious to harshly judge and critique you. First of all, realize that most audience members are on the side of the speaker. Few people go to hear speakers hoping to find fault with them. Most people want to hear a speech that will interest, intrigue, educate, and move them.

In addition to realizing this, you can put friendly faces in the audience. Invite some friends or family members to come hear you speak. Going into the speech, you'll feel better just knowing they'll be there. And when you look up and make eye contact, you'll see familiar faces in the crowd who you know are on your side. You won't feel like it's you versus "them," but more like you're having a conversation with your friends. If it helps, forget about everyone else in the audience and imagine that you *are* having a conversation solely with these friends.

However, you should also force yourself to look at the rest of the audience. If you're nervous about speaking, you might be intimidated about making eye contact and instead keep your eyes planted on your speech. This can make you feel worse, though, because then the audience remains an unknown, faceless, hostile force. If you look at them, you'll see that they're not monsters, just people listening to a speech. More importantly, you'll probably see you've got supporters—people nodding in agreement, taking notes, smiling, or doing something that indicates they're interested in your speech and responding positively. Chances are you'll see several people reacting this way, but even if you only notice one person who does, then you've at least reached someone. Also keep in mind that if one person responded with obvious enthusiasm, others in the audience feel the same way, even if they don't show it quite as blatantly.

REMEMBER WHAT IT'S ALL ABOUT

While giving your speech, you might make yourself feel more anxious by obsessing over your performance. You'll wonder how you're doing and worry about how you sound and look to the audience. Instead of worrying about your delivery, concentrate on your words and the ideas and pieces of information you are sharing.

At one point, when initially writing the speech, these things interested you and meant something to you. Try once again to experience that intellectual and emotional engagement with the topic. As you give your speech, listen to and think about what you are saying, and don't give a second thought to how you are saying it. The speech's content, after all, is what's really important. If you become involved once again with these ideas, you'll be distracted from whatever superficial concerns are making you feel anxious.

THE BIG SECRET

The techniques outlined in this chapter can certainly help cut down on your stage fright, at least to the point where you'll overcome your sense of paralysis and be able to show up and start talking. But chances are your stage fright isn't going to go away completely. Some of it's just a gut response that can't be helped anyway; when you get in front of an audience, you might find your pulse increases, your hands shake a bit, you start to sweat, or your stomach rumbles, and you can't control it.

Here's the biggest secret about public speaking: *No one in the audience can see that you're nervous.* In fact, many people have these same gut responses, even if they've spoken before an audience many times, but they're able to hide it because these symptoms are completely unnoticeable to an audience.

You might think your voice is quavering or that your hand is shaking, but no one in the audience will be able to see or hear it! Even sweating isn't as noticeable as you might think. Audiences might see some sweat on your brow (something you can easily deal with, as we'll see in Chapter 11), but they won't see it on your body. So if you feel like a nervous wreck, just keep on with your speech. You'll be the only one who knows it.

THE SHOW MUST GO ON

Even with all these strategies and techniques, you still might have stage fright. It won't be quite as bad, but it'll still there. Fine. But the show needs to go on. So bite the bullet and go give your speech. The stage fright, nervousness, stress, and anxiety can remain our little secret. Instead, go in acting like a confident and experienced public speaker. Remember, you do have something important to communicate. Your speech that you've thought about and worked so hard to polish to perfection has interesting and important ideas and information in it that people are certain to respond to positively. Once you start speaking, you'll find it's not quite so bad. As you continue, you'll no longer even be aware of our anxiety. And before you know it, it'll be over and you'll be back home relaxing.

11

Grappling with Problems

Our problems are man-made. Therefore they may be solved by man.

—JOHN F. KENNEDY

One of the factors that contributes to the tremendous anxiety people have about public speaking is the fear that something will go wrong. As you prepare your speech—especially if you're not an experienced public speaker—you may find all kinds of nightmarish scenarios running through your mind. This chapter will help alleviate that fear by showing you that just about any problem can easily be conquered.

SWEEPING FOR MINES: ANTICIPATING PROBLEMS

The best way to deal with a problem is to do whatever you can to make certain no problem comes up in the first place. Many of the major things that can go wrong during a speech are easily prevented with a little forethought and preparation.

Think of this process as akin to sweeping for mines. Like soldiers who search the battlefield for deadly land mines to ensure their safe passage, before giving your speech you must assess the situation, look for any potential bombs waiting to explode, and take advanced measures to neutralize them. Then the way will be clear for you to deliver a trouble-free speech.

These are the biggest "mines" that can threaten your speech but can also easily be neutralized beforehand:

Having the Wrong Date, Time, or Location

Fully prepared to give your speech, you arrive at the appointed time and place only to find it empty. If you're lucky, you've come too early and haven't missed your actual speech yet. You might have to return later but at least you'll only have wasted your own time. However, if you've really messed up, you've come too late; while you were sitting around your house thinking you still had plenty of time to prepare, your audience was patiently waiting for you to come deliver your pearls of wisdom.

You might think this scenario seems implausible, but it's actually all too easy for a speaker accidentally to miss his or her own speech. For example, you might have incorrectly noted the date, time, or location in your datebook. There's also the possibility that the time or place has changed since you were originally invited to speak—changes in schedule frequently occur with meetings, conferences, and conventions—and no one notified you or you somehow failed to get the updated information.

This problem is easily avoided by confirming the date, time, and place for your speech sometime before you are scheduled to speak, and then *reconfirming on the day before your speech*. Just be certain you ask someone who does have the correct, most up-to-date information. To be extra safe, you might consult several people, or check to see if there is a printed itinerary or program listing the date, time, and place for your speech.

Getting Lost

In addition to having incorrect information about the date and time, you might also find yourself late because you've had trouble finding the location for your speech. Ironically, there's more of a chance for this to happen with familiar locations, such as in your own home town, where you feel you already know the terrain. In these instances, you might not bother getting directions, only to find when you search for the location it's not exactly where you thought it was.

When you're going to be speaking in an unfamiliar location, you'll usually be provided with or at least know to ask for directions. However, there's then the danger that the directions won't be nearly as straightforward and easy to follow as the person who gave them to you indicated. When you try and follow them yourself, you get hopelessly lost.

Even when you find the right location, it can sometimes be tricky finding the right building, floor, hallway, or room once you get there. Convention centers, for example, are often enormous and mazelike. You might make it to the center itself without trouble, only to find you get lost inside trying to find the right room. If you haven't left yourself enough time for this, you'll show up embarrassingly late at your own speech.

The solution? Go visit the site of your speech at least once before the actual delivery date. Make certain, in addition to finding the general location, you find the *exact* room where the speech will be. That way you'll know exactly where to go on the big day, and how much time it will take you to get there.

Wrong Topic

You've worked hard on writing the perfect speech. You've arrived at the location in plenty of time. You're sitting on the dais, the panel chair introduces you and the topic for your speech. The only trouble is it's completely different from the speech you've actually planned. This nightmare scenario occurs rarely, but it does occur. Miscommunications between you and the event planners, or among the event planners themselves, could be responsible for this kind of mishap.

You can avoid this problem by sending a note or calling someone affiliated with the event and giving them a specific title for your speech. On the day of your speech, you should also make certain that whoever will introduce you has the exact title. It's also worth it to check any official printed itineraries or brochures to make certain your speech is listed with its correct topic.

Missing Materials

The panel chair introduces you, you approach the lectern, smile at the audience, and reach into your jacket pocket for your speech. Too bad it's not there. Instead, at that very moment, it's sitting neatly typed on your desk at home.

This same mishap can occur with any kind of props or special materials that you need for your speech, such as your notes, slides, videos, charts, or hand-outs for the audience. If you need to bring any materials to the speech yourself, leave yourself a reminder to do so. Tape a note to your front door listing the items you need to bring so that on the day of the speech you won't leave the house without seeing it and remembering to bring the necessary items.

If someone else is bringing these materials for you, or if they are being delivered (such as via messenger, or from a copy shop), then call the responsible person and politely remind him or her about what to bring, and when and where the material needs to be there. Tell this person to bring the material at least an hour before your speech is to begin, and then make certain you're there yourself to meet them.

Equipment Foul-Ups

This is the biggie—the problems that most often can foul-up a speech yet are usually easily avoided. Many speeches, as we've discussed, incorporate audiovisual materials and need the necessary equipment. Two problems, though, can occur: One is that the equipment doesn't work; the other is that the equipment isn't even there.

Never assume that equipment will be there without your first requesting it. Seasoned event planners will usually ask you in advance if you require any special equipment, but don't leave it up to them. If you know you'll need some kind of equipment, even if it's just a microphone, make certain you ask for it well in advance. After you've asked for it, ask again. Even if the organizers have told you not to worry about it, claiming that everything is being taken care of, politely remind them at least once about your request as your speech draws closer.

On the day of your speech, go check the equipment yourself. Time and again, speakers are assured their equipment requests are being handled, but somehow the request never goes through. Get to the location early and check the room to make certain everything you requested is there. If not, track down someone organizing the event and have them get it.

While you're at it, check all the equipment you requested to see that it's working properly and that you understand how to work it. Often, particularly at larger venues, there will be an audiovisual technician there to set up and sometimes help you work the equipment. Get there early to meet with this person and go over the operation of each piece of equipment.

Of course, equipment might break down in the middle of your speech, a problem we'll discuss below. However, at the start of your speech, you should at least have taken active measures to ensure that the equipment you want is there and running properly.

SERIAL SWEEPING

In addition to trying to avoid the problems discussed in the preceding section, you should generally think about the event at which you will be speaking and try to anticipate any other possible problems that might arise—and do whatever you can to prevent them. Check and recheck everything, from knowing the right date and time to making certain you have your notes with you to having the equipment you need there and in working order. Then check it all again. You may feel you are being completely neurotic or compulsive, but better that than having a bomb explode in the middle of your speech.

HUMAN ERROR

While many problems like these can be avoided, some come up that just can't be helped. You're only human, after all, and human beings make mistakes. You're also speaking before a live audience. Unlike when you're at home writing a speech, or if you're making a filmed or videotaped presentation, things happen in a live venue that can't be edited out or redone.

Once problems occur, though, you can take action to deal with them. No problem ever has to ruin a speech. In fact, if you take the right measures, most of these problems won't affect the impact of your speech at all.

FLUBBING WORDS AND FEELING TONGUE-TIED

If you've ever seen out-takes from TV shows or movies, you've seen actors flubbing their lines. In those clips, the reaction on their part and that of their costars is usually to break out in hysterical laughter. Take that as a sign of how common it is to miss-peak—even professional actors do it all the time—as well as the lighthearted response people usually have to these errors. Speakers flub words all the time, and their audiences aren't generally bothered by it. However, if you flub a word, you don't want, as those TV actors do, to start laughing hysterically, which would likely get your audience responding the same way. By handling the situation quickly and professionally, you'll move past the mistake, and no one will even remember it.

The most common instance of flubbing words occurs when you say a word similar to the one you meant to (for example, you might say "mural" rather than "morale") or inadvertently switch letters or parts of a word (for example, saying "cativy" instead of "cavity" or saying "comeout" instead of "outcome").

If you catch yourself flubbing a word, simply repeat the word or phrase correctly. Don't apologize or start laughing or cursing yourself. Just fix the mistake and move on. When you repeat the word, say it a bit more slowly and slightly louder to indicate you are conscious of the error and are correcting it, and then proceed with your speech:

> There are three main cagetories . . . CATEGORIES . . .
> that I want to now examine.

If you like, you can preface the correction by saying, "that's" or "or rather":

> This quarter, we have been plagued by plummeting
> pales. . . . rather, plummeting SALES, which is a major
> issue we need to address.

Usually when you flub a word, you'll immediately notice it. Sometimes, though, you may not catch the mistake immediately and will have already continued speaking before you realize it. In that case, you should just continue with the speech. If you stopped at this point to correct yourself, you'd only slow yourself down, draw needless attention to the error, and disrupt the flow of your speech. Rest assured that your audience will still be able to follow your discussion, even if a word or two are mispronounced or misspoken.

However, there might be more serious instances in which you become severely tongue-tied. Rather than merely flubbing a word or two, you might find yourself completely unable to pronounce a word or phrase and instead speaking nonsense. Your own speech suddenly becomes a tongue-twister, and the more you try to continue, the more difficult it is for you to speak.

In this instance you need to take action to get yourself speaking clearly again. Chances are you're becoming tongue-tied because you're speaking too quickly and are too nervous. As soon as you run into this difficulty, stop and take a brief pause. You might even take a sip of water to help calm yourself. Then, look at the words on the page closely and speak them slowly and deliberately. Try speaking these next few words extra slowly and carefully. This will get you past whatever rough patch got you tongue-tied, and as you get back into the rhythm of the speech, you can then pick up your pace to a more normal rate. However, don't pick up the pace too much. Keep your reading rate slow and steady and this will help you avoid becoming tongue-tied again.

SKIPPED LINES AND LOSING YOUR TRAIN OF THOUGHT

If you're reading your speech entirely from the page, you might find you accidentally skip a line, or even a few lines. If you catch this mistake quickly, just pause and go back to the correct line. However, if you've already continued reading for awhile, then just keep going. Your audience should still be able to understand the gist of your discussion.

If you are alternating between reading your notes and speaking directly to your audience, you might at one point lose your place in your notes. If you're having trouble finding the right spot, just say "excuse me for a moment" to the audience and look carefully through your notes. You're better off just taking the time to find the correct place than halfheartedly speaking to the audience while your attention is really on your notes. However, if you really can't find the correct place and are taking too much time, then find something in your notes that you haven't spoken about yet and start discussing it. The speech should still be fine, even if some part of it is missing. As you continue, you may find you remember the sections that you skipped and can return to them.

When speaking directly to an audience, you might also find you suddenly lose your train of thought. You might, for example, be inspired to digress to another topic, or pause to respond to a question, and then forget what you were originally speaking about. If this happens, finish whatever point you are currently making and then refer back to your outline or notes. Try to spot, as quickly as possible, the last section that you had already discussed. If you need to, you can start at the top of your notes or outline and quickly scan down until you find something you haven't yet talked about. If absolutely necessary, you can even ask the audience, "What was I discussing before getting off on this tangent?" It's not the most professional way to get back to your speech, but it's also not horrible, as long as most of your speech is clear and focused.

COUGHING FITS AND FROGS IN THE THROAT

You're successfully delivering your speech in a forceful, powerful manner, when suddenly you begin to get a small tickle in your throat. You try to continue speaking, but the tickle becomes more and more uncomfortable until you need to cough. If that happens, go ahead and cough. You're not going to help anyone trying to choke it back. Cover your mouth, preferably with a handkerchief, cough, and then say "excuse me" to your audience before continuing to speak.

You might also find you get a scratchy or tickling sensation in your throat that makes it difficult to speak. If this happens, say "excuse me" to the audience and slowly take a few sips of water. Don't gulp the water down and immediately start speaking. Slowly sip the water, swallowing carefully. Then wait a moment before beginning to speak again. If you begin speaking and your throat is still scratchy, again say "excuse me" and drink more water. Your audience will be understanding of this delay, as it's something out of your control.

If sipping the water doesn't help, then try popping a cough drop into your mouth. You generally don't want to deliver a speech while sucking on a cough drop; however, if that is the only way you can proceed, go ahead and do it. Purchase the smallest size drops possible, so that you can still speak while it's in your mouth without choking yourself. This means, of course, that you need to bring cough drops with you. For some strange reason, bringing them usually means you won't need them. It's the time you forget them that you'll find you suddenly can't get through your speech without having a coughing fit!

If you typically have a problem with a scratchy throat when speaking, try drinking hot tea with honey and lemon before your speech. This soothes the throat and makes it easier to speak. Also, remember to avoid drinking milk and eating dairy products, as they can irritate the throat and make it difficult to speak clearly.

DON'T SWEAT IT

Some people are more prone to sweating than others, and nervousness can exacerbate the problem. If you want to avoid sweating during a speech, there are certain preventive measures you can take. For instance, you can avoid drinking alcoholic beverages for at least twenty-four hours before a speech, and try to stay away from drinking hot coffee or tea immediately preceding a speech, as they can increase sweating.

Obviously, it's a good idea to avoid getting overheated before your speech. If you're running to make it to your speech on time, or if your speech is on a hot day, there's a good chance you'll arrive sweaty, uncomfortable, and flustered. So go to the location for your speech extra early so that you can relax, give your body time to adjust to the temperature inside the room, and cool down. You might sweat for a few minutes while adjusting, but you can now take the time to go to the bathroom and rinse your face with cold water. By the time you need to speak, you should be cooler and have stopped sweating.

As you wait for your speech, sit calmly, taking deep breaths and occasional sips, but not large quantities, of cool water. Just before your speech is to begin, wipe your brow firmly with a handkerchief. Don't use a paper napkin or tissue, as this can stick to your skin.

Of course, even if you take these preventive measures, you may get up to the lectern and find you begin sweating in the middle of your speech. This might be due to hot lights on you, or it may just be nerves. This situation, though, is easily dealt with.

Since you'll usually be wearing a suit during most speeches and also be standing behind a lectern, no one will really be able to see sweat on your body. However, sweat on your forehead or behind your neck can be uncomfortable and noticeable. Always have a handkerchief in your pocket—not paper tissues. When you feel your brow getting sweaty, use the handkerchief to wipe it dry. Don't timidly dab at it, as this will be pretty ineffectual. Make a firm, decisive swipe, as you continue talking. Your audience will probably be focused on your speech and not even notice your actions. If you like, you can also wait until their attention is focused on some audiovisual prop to wipe your brow. Then no one will even see you do it at all. If you begin to sweat again, go ahead and wipe your brow with the handkerchief again.

NERVOUS STOMACH AND ILLNESS

You might find yourself feeling physically ill or nauseous during a speech. Much of this might be due to nerves, and you can use the techniques and strategies outlined in Chapter 10: Combating Stage Fright to help cut down on the stress and anxiety.

As discussed earlier, avoid eating spicy foods and drinking alcoholic beverages before speaking, as they can contribute to making you feeling sick.

If you are particularly prone to nausea, or if you wake up on the day of your speech feeling mildly sick, go to a drug store or health food store and ask about possible remedies. There are many medicines and all-natural remedies available for coping with nausea. Some can even be taken *before* you feel sick as a preventive measure.

If, however, you wake up on the day of your speech feeling extremely sick, call someone and cancel. It's not likely that you'll feel better by the time your speech is set to begin, and this way you at least give the organizers advance notice.

On the other hand, you might feel fine at the start of your speech and begin to feel sick after you've started talking. If this occurs, do your best to continue. Take deep breaths and sips of cold water when necessary, and read slowly and calmly. As soon as your speech ends, take the event organizer aside and explain that you aren't feeling well and need to leave immediately. However, if you are feeling so sick that you are unable to continue with your speech, don't by any means force yourself to continue. Say "excuse me" to the audience, explain that you'll need to cut the speech short as you're not feeling well, and apologize. If a panel chair or event organizer is present, you can stop your speech and quietly explain the situation to them. They can then explain the situation to the audience.

AUDIOVISUAL EQUIPMENT PROBLEMS

As noted previously, you should check and double-check all the audiovisual equipment you plan to use for your speech beforehand. However, even if you check everything and it's working fine, you might find that at the point when you actually need it during your speech, suddenly it's not working. Audiovisual equipment is notorious for breaking down at the most inappropriate times and for inexplicable reasons. Sometimes the equipment can seem downright temperamental, working fine one moment and then frozen the next for no apparent reason.

The first thing to do is to stay calm. Pause, take a breath, and look carefully at the equipment and think about whatever you are currently doing. Quickly check for the obvious—that the plug is in, that you are pushing the correct buttons and using the proper remote control—and try to operate the equipment again. If it still doesn't work, don't continue trying to fix it yourself. Stop what you are doing and, if there is a technician present, calmly ask him or her to come check the equipment. If no such technician is available, ask if there is anyone in the room who is familiar with this kind of equipment and can come check it out.

Whatever you do, do not have an outburst over this. This is not the time or place to get into a fight with the technician or event planners, blaming them for the mishap, or for having a temper tantrum and throwing equipment across the room. The foul-up might very well make you feel like having a tantrum, but you must not let the audience see that. Continue with your speech and, if possible, make a joke about the situation. Show the audience you are still very much in control of the situation, and that this minor foul-up ultimately has no impact on the overall power of your speech.

While someone else is trying to fix the equipment, continue with your speech. You don't want this foul-up to create a long delay. That will tire your audience, and you'll have difficulty getting their attention again afterwards. As you get to sections of your speech that refer to the audiovisual props, either skip those sections, or describe whatever prop or image you would have shown them at this point. For example, if you were planning to show slides of an advertising campaign, do your best to describe some of the images to the audience. If you were going to show a graph or chart, summarize whatever data it documented.

However, if the attempt to fix the equipment is disruptive and distracts the audience from your speech, you should consider not bothering with it. You are better off having the audience pay attention to your speech, even if the audiovisuals need to be cut out, than not listening to you because there's too much other activity in the room. Your words should remain the focus of the speech. If you decide not to bother with fixing the equipment, thank the person for trying to help, and explain that you will continue speaking without it.

If the equipment *is* fixed, you'll then need to make a decision about whether or not to go back to show the audience whatever you had planned to during the earlier parts of your speech. If you can do so quickly, without having to repeat your entire speech, then do it. You will have to briefly remind the audience what you are showing them and quickly explain how it applies to your speech. If the prop or image requires too much explanation, then don't bother going back to it. Continue with your speech and start incorporating whatever additional audiovisual elements now come up.

SOUND PROBLEMS

As we noted earlier, if you are speaking to a large audience or in a large room, you're going to want to use a microphone. As with all your audiovisual equipment, you'll want to check beforehand that the microphone is there and that it works.

When you go up to speak, adjust the microphone to the right height and ask the audience if they can hear you. If not, you may have to readjust the microphone so that it better picks up your words. You also might need to have someone adjust the volume level.

As you speak, you may find you have difficulties with the sound, such as static, drastic changes in volume level, or annoying feedback. If this occurs, ask if there's anyone present who can fix the problem. If they can do so quickly, wait for them to fix the problem before speaking. If no one is present to work on the problem, or if it can't be fixed quickly, you should try to proceed without it. This means you'll have to work hard to project your voice. It might be somewhat of a strain on you, but you should be able to speak loudly enough for most people in the room to be able to hear you.

Tell the audience you're proceeding without the microphone, and ask them if they can hear you speak now without it. Ask people in the back row to raise their hands if they can hear you. If no one raises their hands, try speaking even louder and asking again. You should be able to raise the volume of your voice, without necessarily having to scream, so that people can hear you at a distance. If possible, you might ask people in the back to move closer to you.

If you try projecting your voice loudly and still can't make yourself heard, tell the audience there will be a brief delay while the problem is fixed. Then find someone to take care of the problem. Unlike a problem with audiovisual equipment, a speech can't continue if people can't hear you. In this circumstance, you're better off stopping and getting the microphone fixed than trying to proceed.

TIME RUNNING OUT

Earlier we discussed the importance of meeting whatever time restrictions are given to you for your speech, as well as ways to edit your speech beforehand to fit that time allotment. However, you may find when you get to the actual speech, you still find time running out before you are finished speaking. For example, you might be speaking at a different rate than you did when practicing the speech at home. If the person before you went over their time, you might also find you have less time to speak than you had anticipated.

The worst thing that could happen is that you are told by the panel chair or MC, in the middle of your speech, that you must now stop speaking. This not only makes you look bad in front of the audience, but it also means you won't get an opportunity to make your most impressive points and powerful concluding statements.

The best way to handle this problem is to see it coming. As mentioned earlier, keep a watch propped on the lectern facing you. You don't need to be obsessive about the time; just quickly glance at the watch every few minutes. You particularly want to check the time after you've reached the halfway point in your speech. You should, if everything is going well, reach the halfway point when half the time is left. If not, you can make adjustments, such as slightly increasing the rate at which you are speaking. However, you don't want to increase your rate too much, as you want the audience to be able to understand you easily. Instead, you might consider skipping parts of the speech that are not as important, or summarizing certain sections.

You want to make certain, though, that you have time to read your concluding remarks in their entirety. Remember, this is the part of the speech you've worked particularly hard on because it makes such a lasting impression on the audience. If you see that you only have five minutes left, and you still have plenty more of your speech to go, summarize as much as you can and then read your concluding remarks. This will provide you with a much stronger finish than if you were forced to end mid-speech.

SPEECH RUNNING UNDER

A far less serious although far more common problem is finding your speech falling short of the time allotment. This occurs frequently because speakers get a bit nervous and then tend to read faster during the real speech than they did when practicing. You probably won't even realize you're speaking faster than normal, because you'll be so concerned about other factors. Again, discreetly keep your eye on the time to see how quickly you are running through the speech and make adjustments to your speaking rate. Take special note of the halfway point. If you find that half the time is up and you've already gone well beyond the halfway point of your speech, then slow yourself down. Don't slow yourself down so much, though, that it becomes too noticeable or strange.

If you finish your speech and time is left, ask if there are any questions. (Advice for handling question-and-answer sessions is addressed in Chapter 12 Roleplaying). Generally, question-and-answer sessions can easily take up whatever time remains.

DISRUPTIONS

If you're not used to speaking in front of a live audience, you may not realize how much noise audiences make. While you're speaking, you'll be somewhat aware of shuffling and shifting in your audience as people reach into their briefcases for tissues, crinkle notepaper, shift in their seats, etc. This doesn't mean they're not listening to you. Even with the most engaging of speakers, there is going to be some movement and minor noise in the crowd. However, sometimes a more blatant disruption will distract the rest of the audience from you. You'll then have to take action.

Common disruptions during a speech include latecomers trying to find a seat and people whispering among themselves. Most of these disruptions are short-lived and rather minor, and therefore not worth bothering about. In the time it would take for you to stop your speech and deal with the disruption, they would probably have stopped doing whatever was disruptive in the first place.

However, there are instances in which these disruptions can become more distracting. Sometimes a latecomer, rather than quickly and quietly finding a seat, will climb over people, talking and making noise, and distracting many people in your audience. Similarly, if people are whispering loudly and show no signs of stopping, you also will want to do something about it. The best way to initially handle the situation is to stop speaking and look at whomever is causing the disruption. They might not at first realize that you are focusing on them, but as the room becomes quiet, they should figure it out. In many cases, other people in the audience will alert them to the fact that you are waiting for them to get quiet. Once made aware that they've been disruptive, these people usually will quickly stop what they are doing and pay attention to you. You can then continue speaking.

If pausing and staring at the disruptive person doesn't work, then you will have to say something polite but firm, such as, "Please take the nearest seat so I can continue" or "Would you mind taking your conversation outside so I can continue?"

Usually direct comments like these will do the trick. If not, more drastic measures might need to be taken. In these instances, the disruption becomes more along the lines of heckling.

Hecklers are audience members who insist on speaking during your speech, usually to voice some kind of criticism. Sometimes the heckling won't necessarily be critical, merely an audience member who insists on sharing his or her opinion on the subject immediately.

Heckling can be a major disruption during a speech, one that particularly causes anxiety among speakers. It doesn't, however, occur all that often, and chances are you won't have to deal with this problem. In most instances, audience members will politely listen to you speak, and save any criticism or comments for later on, when they can talk with you in private.

Sometimes, an audience member will stick their hand in the air and wait for you to call on them. It's not a good idea to do this, though, as it will cut time from your speech and disrupt the flow of your argument. Usually if you ignore the hand, the person will become tired and put it down. However, sometimes they might only begin to wave it more frantically. When the hand becomes a major distraction, you should then take action. Simply say to the person, "I'll take questions at the end, thank you."

If a person in the audience refuses to put their hand down, or if they begin to make loud comments during your speech, you need to take firm and immediate action. Start by first pausing and staring at the person, without continuing your speech. Often that will be enough to get them to stop talking, or to get other audience members to tell them to be quiet. If that doesn't work, try being polite. Tell them they'll have an opportunity to share their opinion after the speech, and that you would appreciate their being quiet for now.

If those two methods fail, then you need to be more direct in your comments. Tell the person that you simply cannot continue speaking with these disruptions. Remind them that you are the one who was invited to speak before the audience, not them. Ask the audience who they would rather hear speak at this point, you or the heckler. Usually that will be enough to get other audience members, or the event planners, involved in getting this person to be quiet. If not, you should ask someone in charge of the event to handle the problem.

Good event planners should be in control of the situation. If someone is disrupting your speech, these people should take some active measures to quiet or evict the heckler so that you can continue. If they don't, then as a last measure, you should announce that you refuse to continue until you have the audience's full attention, and then take your seat. If that still doesn't put an end to the disruptive behavior, then you shouldn't feel obligated to continue speaking. Why should you put yourself in an uncomfortable situation, when you've been the one invited to come speak? It's just not worth continuing in this kind of adverse situation.

Sometimes, though, you may be giving a speech before a crowd who you know in advance will be hostile to you or critical of your ideas. If you know this in advance, you can take measures from the start to try to alleviate the disruptions. Announce at the beginning of the speech that you realize your ideas may not be popular here, and that you are happy to discuss and debate them, as well as hear other points of view. But tell them that you first want to be able to present your view in its entirety, before opening up the floor to debate. Thank the audience in advance for this courtesy. You may, in this situation, want to keep your speech on the brief side. Usually the audience will let you speak for a short time about something with which they don't agree. If you continue for too long, though, they'll become angry and more vocal.

IT'S UP TO YOU

You've just read about the various problems that might arise during a speech. Don't let this make you feel anxious though. Especially if you take precautions described in previous chapters, your speech will most likely be glitch-free. And if a problem does occur, you can use one of these strategies to handle it. But remember, you have to be the one to take action. When you are the speaker, you're the one in control, so you've got to deal with whatever problem arises. Don't be concerned that a problem means your speech is utterly ruined. When a problem is handled quickly and correctly by a speaker, it's usually forgotten by everyone in the audience. And in some instances, it can even work to your advantage. Your successful handling of a problem, showing an audience that you are a confident and composed speaker, might even make them think more highly of you.

12

Roleplaying: Additional Speaker Responsibilities and Special Circumstances

*Perhaps one never seems so much at one's ease
as when one has to play a part.*

—OSCAR WILDE

Being a public speaker sometimes involves doing a lot more than giving a speech. There are various roles you might be called upon to play in varying circumstances in which you'll have additional responsibilities. As with giving a speech, it's important in these instances that you know what you're in for, and take the time to plan for it. This chapter outlines the specific responsibilities you'll face with these various roles and special circumstances—and shows how to prepare for and pull them off without a hitch.

QUESTION-AND-ANSWER SESSIONS

Many speeches are followed by a question-and-answer period during which people in the audience are invited to ask the speaker questions. These questions usually are directly related to specific points raised in the speech, although they also can stem from the speech's general subject area. You'll have two important jobs to do during this session: listening to the questions and then responding to them.

Making Sense of the Questions

When the floor is opened to questions, either you or a panel chair will call on people in the audience who raise their hands to indicate they have a question. Don't be concerned if at first no one raises a hand. It sometimes takes a few moments for people to formulate questions or to decide to raise their hand. Once one person raises their hand and asks a question, usually several others will follow. If you do wait a minute and no one raises their hand, thank the audience for listening and go sit down. Almost always, though, there will be many hands raised.

Look, Listen, Repeat: When the person asks a question, make certain you look directly at him or her and listen very carefully to the question. Although this sounds like an obvious point, you might be surprised how easy it is to let your mind wander during these Q and A sessions. After you finish speaking, you'll be feeling drained, and tempted to sit back, relax, and think back about the speech, wondering how it went. If you do, though, you might miss the question and have to ask the person to repeat it, which can cause resentment on the part of the entire audience, who might interpret your lack of attention as lack of interest in their responses to your speech. So make certain you put your own thoughts and emotions on hold and really listen to the question. However, if you can't hear the question, you can then certainly ask the person to repeat it louder.

After the person has asked a question, you should then repeat it out loud yourself. You don't necessarily need to repeat it word for word, but try to summarize it as accurately as possible. This will enable everyone in the audience to hear the question, which many might not be able to do. It will also give you a brief moment to compose your thoughts about what you would like to say in response, as well as indicate if you have properly understood the question being asked of you.

Confusing Questions: If you don't understand a question, ask the person to rephrase it or clarify it. After they do, if you still don't understand it, don't take up any more time trying to get this person to better articulate their question. Try to formulate some brief, general remark that relates to some part of their question or to something you think their question was at least trying to address. Then move on to another question. People in the audience will appreciate it that you didn't take up everyone's time dealing with some overly cryptic question.

Irrelevant Questions: Similarly, if you do understand the question but don't find it very relevant to your speech or topic, don't feel compelled to answer it. You might first make some kind of compliment so that the questioner will not feel insulted, such as saying it's an interesting question to consider. Then explain that, as you can't see how the question is relevant to the current discussion, you'd prefer to move on to another question. Most people in the audience will appreciate that you keep the discussion focused on a specific topic.

No Question Asked: Very often, you'll find that people use a question-and-answer session as a forum to share their own opinions on some subject without ever actually asking a question. This can be a problem because it will take up too much time and prevent others from asking real questions. It will also irritate others in the audience, who might not be at all interested in this random person's opinion.

If you call on someone and they begin making their own speech without apparently building to a question, feel free to politely interrupt them and say, "I'm, sorry, what's your question here?" If they do have a question, your interruption should prompt them to ask it.

However, if they don't have a question and say that they simply wanted to make a comment or share their view, tell them that you'd be happy to talk with them after the session but want to keep this time open just for questions. Don't wait for a response from them; immediately ask for more questions from the audience, which should put a stop to this person's commentary.

Lengthy Questions: A similar problem occurs when someone does ask a question, but it is a rather lengthy one with various parts to it. You can interrupt them early on and tell them you'd like to first answer one particular part of the question. Another option is to let the person deliver their entire question, or series of questions, and then respond only to parts of it. Focus on whatever seems most relevant to your speech or that you feel most confident about responding to. When your response is finished, call on someone else. Chances are no one will notice or mind that you haven't answered the person's entire question.

Your Response to Questions

Once a question has been posed to you and you've repeated it back to the audience, you then have to respond to it. In some ways, this makes the question-and-answer session more of a challenge than giving the speech itself. For the speech, you had time to think, prepare, and polish your words to perfection. For the question-and-answer period, though, you'll have to think on your feet and present a response without any extensive preparation.

Don't think, though, that people expect the same kind of perfectly polished, comprehensive, and logical kind of discussion as your speech provided. Most people understand that a question-and-answer session is more informal and won't mind if your response is more loosely structured and less refined than your speech.

Generally, people will ask questions because they genuinely want to know more about some point or piece of information you raised in your speech, or merely want something clarified. You'll usually know the answer to their question and be able to respond without much problem.

Short and Simple Responses: Keep your answers short and to the point. This will enable other people to have an opportunity to ask questions, and it will also make you sound much more articulate. It's too difficult to improvise a long speech on the spot that is also clearly organized and focused. If a response goes on too long, inevitably it is going to sound jumbled or repetitive and be very difficult for the audience to follow. On the other hand, a short response of only a few sentences is easier to keep focused on a specific point and will be more understandable to the audience. So keep your answers short and sweet.

Preparing Responses in Advance: You also don't need to think of yourself as entering a Q and A session completely unprepared. In the course of preparing your speech, you immersed yourself in and studied up on the subject matter. If you have succeeded in making yourself something of an expert in the subject, you should be able to respond to most questions related to it.

At the same time, you *can* prepare specific responses for a Q and A session in advance. As you work on and rehearse your speech, try to guess possible questions that someone might ask. You can then think about and even talk through your likely response to these questions. If these questions do come up, you'll be all set.

Of course, these exact questions might not come up; however, the questions that are raised might be similar enough to the ones you've thought about that you can still use parts of the responses you've already prepared. You can also try to find a way to segue from the question asked of you to a response you've already prepared. This is a particularly effective method for avoiding a question you don't like, enabling you instead to address a topic you feel more comfortable discussing. You simply need to come up with a quick transitional statement to get off the question and onto your preferred topic, such as:

"That question raises another really important issue . . ."
"I think what's really at issue here is . . ."
"Let me try to get at that question by first addressing this . . ."

If You Don't Know the Answer: If you don't know the answer to the question, it's fine for you to admit that. Whatever you do, don't try to fake a response. Someone will figure out you're wrong and it will only make you look bad. Your speech will have already demonstrated to the audience that you are an intelligent, knowledgeable person regarding this topic, even if you can't answer this particular question. It's okay for you not to know everything, and no one really expects that you will. Most people respect someone who admits it when they don't know something; no one respects someone who tries to con their way through a phony answer.

In this situation, you might even ask if anyone else in the audience knows the answer to the question. The audience will like that you respect their intelligence and expertise. If someone in the audience does pipe up and announce they do know something about this particular question, smile, thank them for sharing the information, and comment on how it's always interesting to learn something new.

Don't Get Defensive: Sometimes someone will use their question as a means of critiquing or attacking your speech. Do not by any means get yourself involved in an argument or debate with someone from the audience. This might irritate the audience by taking up their time, and it can damage your credibility. You are the invited speaker, and you don't necessarily have to justify your views in front of everyone. Simply thank this person for sharing their opinion, and call on someone else. If they persist in their inquiry, tell them you would be happy to talk to with them further after the session, but you want to have time to respond to other people's questions. Most of the audience will respond positively to this, as you appear to be considering their interests.

BEING A PANELIST

Many speeches are given as part of a panel centering on some specific topic. A panel consists of several speakers and a panel chair. Usually the speakers each prepare their own speech, and take turns delivering their individual speeches in their entirety. Some panels, though, are more open-ended discussions, in which the chair poses questions to panel members, or takes questions from audience members directed at the panel.

Advance Considerations and Preparations

If you are invited to sit on a panel, find out if you are expected to prepare an entire speech, or if it will be a more open discussion. If you are to give a speech, make certain you find out how much time you are allotted. Most panels follow a tight schedule so that all panelists will have equal time. In this instance, you particularly want to make certain that you write and edit your speech to fit the time limit, as it's rude to cut into another panelist's time.

You should also ask who the other panelists are and try to find out about their backgrounds before meeting them in person. Very often, sitting on a panel can be a prime networking opportunity, enabling you to initiate a professional relationship with someone else in your field. By knowing something about the other panelists, you can then open up a conversation with them.

More importantly, this advance information about the other panelists can help you avoid an unnecessarily uncomfortable situation. For example, if you learn that someone else on the panel is a world-renowned expert in a particular area, you might decide to avoid giving a speech on that subject. Similarly, if your speech espouses a particular viewpoint that you know others on the panel actively and openly oppose, you can at least be ready for some kind of debate and have a strong defense for your speech prepared in advance.

Bring Your Own Bio

It's usually the panel chair's responsibility to contact you sometime before the panel to find out the topic and title of your speech as well as some information about you to use when introducing you. As with other forms of speeches, you should offer to provide the host with your own brief biography, and bring an extra copy to the panel.

Show Respect

When sitting on a panel, make certain you are always polite to and respectful of the other panelists, even if you disagree with some of their ideas. When other people are delivering their speeches, be sure you pay attention to them—and that you *look* like you're paying attention to them. Don't ever do anything to disrupt another person's speech, such as staring out the window, looking impatient, or flipping through pages in your notepad. Keep in mind that the audience will be able to see what you're doing during the other person's speech; if you look attentive, you'll make a positive impression. By treating others with courtesy and respect, you convey an air of professionalism that can greatly influence people's impressions of you.

When the panel is over, you may want to talk with the other panelists about their speeches. Again, even if you don't agree, try to find something positive to say, such as that you found it interesting or well written. This can help forge a valuable professional connection.

During a Discussion

If the panel is a more open discussion, again make certain you pay attention and listen carefully to the other panelists when they speak. It's generally a good idea to avoid interrupting others while they are speaking, as this can seem rude and egotistical. However, you might find that you then never get to take part in the discussion. If you do interrupt someone else, do it as politely as possible. Say, "Excuse me, but if I can just jump in here. . . " and then begin speaking.

Throughout a discussion, make certain you act calmly and treat others with respect, even if you disagree with them. Don't try to persuade the other panelists to see things your way. No panelist is ever going to change his or her view in front of an entire audience. The best you can do is to win over individuals in the audience, and to do that you need to make a positive impression on them. Avoid having any kind of emotional outburst or getting into a heated debate or screaming match, which can give the audience a negative impression of you regardless of what you say. Keep a cool head the entire time and calmly and clearly communicate your views and opinion.

CHAIRING A PANEL

In addition to serving on a panel, you might be invited to chair a panel. If you are a panel chair, it's your responsibility to make certain the entire session runs smoothly.

Advance Preparations

Make certain you contact each panelist in advance and remind them of the date, time, and place. You should also inform them of their time allotment and politely ask them to please abide by it so that everyone on the panel will have equal time. Ask if they'll be needing any special audiovisual equipment so you can arrange for it to be there for them.

You should also ask them if they would mind preparing a brief biography for you to read when you introduce them. If they do not want to do this, you can ask them to send you a resume or CV (curriculum vitae) from which you can cull relevant information. It is helpful to type up a short introduction for each speaker in advance. This will make your duties much simpler when you chair the panel. You can simply read the biographies you've already prepared. As you would in preparing your own biography, include the person's professional background and experience, highlighting anything that particularly relates to the panel. (There's more information about introducing speakers in the following section.)

Before the day of the panel session, send each panelist an itinerary, listing who will be speaking and in what order. Include the date, time, and place on this sheet to serve as a final reminder.

The day of the session, make certain you get to the location extra early. Check out the room to be sure it is clean and set up properly. Usually you'll want to arrange the room with the audience facing the panelists, who sit at a long table at the front of the room. If panelists will be delivering speeches, there should be a lectern at which they can stand. If the room is large, you'll also want to provide a microphone. As a courtesy to the panel, arrange to have pitchers of water on the table. If panelists plan on using audiovisual equipment, make certain everything is there and working properly.

As the panelists arrive, personally greet each one and introduce yourself. Check to see that there have been no changes in their speech's title or topic. Show them where they should sit, and remind them of the order in which they will speak. You should also remind them of their time allotment, politely telling them that you need to make certain there is enough time for each panelist to give their speech as well as to take questions at the end. You might also want to tell them that when they have five minutes left, you will signal them.

Playing Host

When the panel begins, you as the chair should think of yourself as the host or M.C. It's your job to keep everything running smoothly. You should start out by briefly introducing yourself by name and then welcoming everyone in the audience to the panel. Make certain you introduce the title, theme, or topic of the panel. To introduce each panelist, simply read the brief bio they gave you or that you prepared in advance. When they come up the lectern, shake their hand and then take your own seat. While each person is reading, you should be fully focused on them and listening attentively.

After each person concludes their speech, come up to the lectern. You can again shake the speaker's hand, and whisper some compliment, such as "well done" or "thank you." Don't, however, make any kind of remarks about the speech to the audience. It's not your place as the chair to offer editorial commentary about the speeches, and you don't want to offend any of the panelists by complimenting some and not others. Just proceed with the next person's introduction.

Watching the Time

While listening to the speeches, you should also carefully watch the time. When there are five minutes remaining, try to quietly signal the speaker by catching his or her eye and pointing to your watch. Don't, however, cut them off from speaking. Give them another minute or two to see if they are coming to a close.

If they go more than a few minutes past their allotment and don't seem to be coming to a close, then you should politely interrupt them, announcing that time is up, and ask them now to make their conclusion. This shouldn't offend them as you are still giving them an opportunity to conclude. They should then quickly wrap up their speech. If they don't, you then can cut them off and move on to the next panelist, saying, "I'm sorry, but we're well over the time allotment now, and we have to get to the next panelist. Thank you for speaking."

Dealing with Disturbances

If there are any kinds of major disruptions or disturbances during the speeches—such as people talking without stopping or hecklers—it's your job to take care of the situation. If necessary, interrupt the speaker to ask these people to be quiet. You can also tell hecklers that if they can't keep their comments to themselves until after the panel, then they'll have to leave.

Chairing Q & A Sessions

After the last speaker has gone, you might open the floor for questions. Question-and-answer sessions are usually included as parts of panels, and they generally follow all of the speeches, rather than coming after each individual speaker. Usually the chair calls on individuals in the audience, who direct their question to a specific panelist. Try to call on a variety of people in the audience. Audience members might become resentful if you call on the same person more than once when others haven't had a chance to ask their own questions.

You as the chair should repeat the question so that everyone can hear it, and announce to whom the question was directed. As the chair, you might also have to actively intervene to make certain people do ask questions that clearly relate to some topic. If you hear people begin to make their own speeches, or formulating overly complicated, lengthy questions, prompt them to get to their exact question.

Make certain that you set a time limit to the question-and-answer session as well. When the time is almost up, announce that you'll take one more question. After the last question has been answered, thank everyone for attending, and the panelists for speaking. Try to finish with a sincere, but general, compliment about all the speakers, such as "Those were all really fascinating speeches. Thank you."

Facilitating an Open Discussion

If your duty as panel chair involves facilitating a more open discussion among the panelists, come prepared with a list of provocative questions related to the panel topic. Try to brainstorm about ten questions; to guarantee that the questions will generate discussion, make certain they are open-ended, inviting many possible responses. Type them up on a single sheet of paper that you bring with you to the panel.

After briefly introducing each of the panelists to the audience, start with your first question, and see what kind of discussion it generates. Usually one of the panelists will jump in and begin to respond; in turn, the other panelists will probably then contribute their view or provide some kind of counter-argument.

You may not get to all of the questions you prepared, nor should you try to get to all of them. If the questions are good ones, then they should generate plenty of interesting discussion. As long as the discussion progresses, don't feel the need to keep asking questions. When you sense a lull in the discussion, or if the responses become repetitive, then turn to another question on your list. Based on the direction the discussion goes, you might also be inspired to improvise new questions.

It's important that you make certain all the panelists are participating. Some speakers might be intimidated about interrupting others. If you find that a panelist is not getting an opportunity to speak, you can turn to them and ask what their opinion is regarding the current topic under discussion. Usually they'll welcome this invitation to speak.

If you are familiar with each panelist's background or area of expertise, you might also try to generate questions that are specifically directed to each person. You should first give that particular person a chance to respond to the question you designed for him or her. When that panelist is finished speaking, you can then ask if any of the other panelists would like to reply. When you organize the discussion this way, make certain you direct at least one question to each panelist.

While you do want to generate an interesting discussion, it's important that it not become too chaotic, with too many panelists speaking at once and the audience unable to hear any of them. If this happens, you should step in to establish some kind of order. Ask the panelists to speak one at a time so that the audience can hear them. You might even announce the order in which each person will now get a chance to speak. Simply say something like, "Let's hold on a second. We need to slow down so the audience can hear you. Let's start with Professor Anderson; then we'll hear from Ms. Stern, and then from Dr. Clark."

To conclude the panel discussion, you might invite each panelist to offer some kind of final statement. Just make certain these comments are brief and stick to the topic. You don't want this to become a series of long speeches.

INTRODUCING A KEYNOTE SPEAKER

When chairing a panel, as we've seen, your duties include briefly introducing each speaker. In this instance, you need to keep the introductions relatively short so as to give the panelists enough time for their own speeches. It would also be rather boring for an audience to have to listen to three or four lengthy introductions during one panel session.

However, there are occasions when you will need to prepare a slightly longer, more detailed introduction, particularly when the entire event centers on one guest or keynote speaker. For these longer introductions, you have two important goals: the first is to introduce the speaker to the audience, providing relevant details about his or her background and experience; the second is preparing the audience for the speech. Your role is somewhat akin to an opening act at a concert; you get the audience in the right mood and in the right frame of mind for the next "performer."

Although these introductions will be longer than those for panel speakers, they should still not be very long. You never want the introduction to take the same amount of time as the speech itself! Instead, it should take up a fraction of the overall time. A formal introduction never really needs to be longer than five minutes.

To prepare a long introduction, it's important that you have enough information about this speaker to include specific details. If you don't know the person yourself, make certain you do research to learn more about him or her. Request a resume or CV, and interview the person's colleagues. If the person has published books or articles, try to read some of them. It's also a good idea for you to talk with the speaker in person. In addition to asking the speaker which points he or she would like you to emphasize in your introduction, try to have a more casual conversation; this will help you get a sense of his or her personality and also might reveal some more interesting information than you'd get from a resume. Ask the speaker to tell you about what he or she plans to say in the speech, or to provide you with an advance copy of it. Having a sense of the speech's content will help you write an introduction that correctly introduces both the speaker and the topic.

You should take time to plan, write, and rehearse this kind of introduction, just as you would for a speech you are giving yourself. You can follow the same three-part structure we discussed in the last section of the book.

Start the introduction with a hook to get the audience's attention. Avoid clichés (such as "this person needs no introduction") and uninteresting openings, such as announcing the person's name and title. Instead, start out with a really interesting piece of information about this speaker, such as a description of one of their more spectacular achievements or experiences, or an anecdote about them you heard from a friend or colleague, or an account of one of your own encounters with this person.

After the hook, you should then more formally introduce the speaker and the specific topic of the speech. Introduce the speaker by full name and, if appropriate, a professional title. *Make certain you know how to pronounce the speaker's name correctly.* You can ask the speaker yourself, as long as you do it in advance and in private. They won't be insulted by this, but they might be if you mispronounced their name in front of the entire audience.

After the formal introduction, you can proceed to outline the speaker's background and various achievements and experiences. However, since this introduction will be longer than those for a panel discussion, you need to make this description of the person more interesting and varied to hold the audience's attention. In a shorter introduction, you can simply list the person's background much as it appears on their resume. But for a longer introduction that would quickly become boring and repetitive. Rather than just listing the speaker's experience, try to also include anecdotes or quotations (from the speaker or their colleagues), which will make for a more varied, colorful introduction.

If you know the speaker yourself, you can also relate some of your personal experiences with him or her. However, the introduction should not be about you and your achievements. Only talk about yourself if it somehow relates to the speaker.

Anything you say about the speaker in this introduction should be accurate and sincere. Don't talk about your enormous respect and admiration of this person if you've only just heard of them.

In addition to covering the speaker's background and experience, you can also briefly describe or refer to the topic of the speech. You need to be careful, though, not to steal the speaker's thunder. It's not your job to deliver an entire speech, and you don't want to cover the same material the speaker will. Instead, you might discuss why this speaker has been invited to discuss this particular topic. Does it have some timely significance or special importance? Is it especially significant to this particular audience? How might the audience go on to use the information the speaker will be sharing with them

Although you can discuss the topic of the speech, don't tell the audience how they should respond to it. For example, don't tell them they're certain to be fascinated or moved by this speech, which might actually make them wonder if the speech really *is* so fascinating or moving. Give the audience the freedom to figure out for themselves how they'll respond.

It's also extremely important that the tone of your introduction be appropriate for the speech that is to follow. Remember, your role is to put the audience in the proper mood and frame of mind for the speech. For example, if the speaker is going to address a very serious issue, you should not include any jokes or humorous stories in your introduction but make it appropriately somber. On the other hand, if the speech is to be a more lighthearted one, your introduction can certainly be humorous. However, never use humor at the expense of the speaker, even if you are speaking in jest.

At the conclusion of your introduction, you should formally introduce the speaker. Again, give his or her full name, professional title, and the title of the speech. You can preface this formal introduction with an introductory phrase such as, "And now, it is my great pleasure to introduce to you. . . ." Wait for the speaker to approach the lectern, and make certain you shake his or her hand. Then take your own seat and listen attentively to the speech.

BEING AN M.C. OR HOST

For certain occasions you might be asked to serve as a master of ceremonies or host. This person oversees an entire event from start to finish, usually one at which there are various speakers or activities, such as a meal, music and entertainment, and toasts.

Being a host or M.C. is somewhat akin to being a panel chair. It's your job to make certain the entire event runs smoothly, and to introduce each of the various speakers. In addition to introducing speakers, you might also have to introduce the various activities. You might, for example, announce when it is time to eat, or introduce some form of entertainment.

As the host or M.C. you are instrumental in setting the tone for the entire event, and your tone should match that of the occasion. Usually these will be more socially oriented events, so you can be more casual and personable than you might be at a serious panel discussion. You don't need to plan any formal speeches or introductions in advance. Instead, keep it more casual and chatty. Try to make everyone feel welcome and encourage them to enjoy themselves, as if they are guests in your own home.

Before the event, make certain you receive an itinerary listing the various speakers and/or activities. If you are going to be introducing speakers, be sure you have brief biographies of each of them.

At the start of the event, welcome everyone and tell them a little about what the event will be like. Then introduce the first activity or speaker. Each time you take the stage to speak again, you should say something. Either tell a story or a joke, or give an introduction to the next activity or speaker. None of these interludes should be very long and they don't need to be carefully scripted. Your role is to keep the entire event moving along smoothly and to give it some unity.

At the conclusion of the event, you should offer some kind of final remark to let everyone know the event is over and they can go home. You might, for example, now thank those who organized and participated in the event.

RUNNING A MEETING

Running a meeting is again somewhat like chairing a panel. It's your job to make certain the entire event runs smoothly and on schedule. You should always have an agenda for the meeting set in advance. You might decide on the agenda yourself, or various people might play a part in determining it. If you are the one running the meeting, though, you must have the final agenda in your hand. It's a good idea to send all those attending the meeting a copy of this agenda, along with a reminder of the date and time the meeting is to take place. If various people are to speak or make presentations at the meeting, make certain they know in advance what will be expected of them so they can prepare.

You might want to arrive early to arrange the room a particular way. Generally meetings run better if everyone can sit around some kind of table. That way, as different people speak, everyone will be able to see and hear them. If no table is available, you might arrange the chairs in a circle before people arrive, so that they'll sit facing one another. If the meeting is too large to work around a table or in a circle, you may then need to arrange it more like a formal lecture, with everyone facing a lectern at which each speaker will stand when it's his or her turn. You might also want to arrange for paper, pens, pitchers of water, and coffee or refreshments.

Start the meeting promptly. Depending on the nature of the meeting you may want to begin with a brief welcome and by thanking everyone for attending. At a more informal meeting, especially one where people don't know each other, you might also begin by going around the room and having everyone introduce themselves and perhaps tell something about themselves. However, at more professionally oriented meetings, you probably can dispense with these introductory pleasantries. Attending a meeting is part of these people's professional duties; they didn't have any choice about whether or not to attend, so thanking them for coming would seem insincere.

Instead you can start the meeting by getting right to business. Start by announcing the overall purpose and/or specific aims for that day's meeting. As you call on various people to make a report or to speak, it's unnecessary to provide a lengthy introduction for them. At most meetings, people will already know one another. Instead, announce the person's name and what they will now discuss. For example, you might say something like, "And now we'll hear from Sharon Gold about how the new marketing plan is progressing."

Try to keep the meeting on a tight schedule so that it will end close to the time you announced it would. The attendees probably scheduled their time around the meeting and might have other commitments; if you run late, they'll begin to get impatient and fidgety.

If you find that particular issues generate extensive discussion at the meeting, or that you don't have enough time to get to certain items on the agenda, you might want to plan another meeting. At the present meeting, you can set a date and time for that future one.

Before you close the meeting, ask if there's anything else important that needs to be addressed at this present time. If someone raises an issue that requires extensive discussion, see if it can be put off to the next meeting.

PRESENTING AN AWARD/ACCEPTING AN AWARD

An award presentation is a form of a personal homage. Like all personal homages, it needs to be accurate, detailed, and sincere. You should of course say positive things about the person being honored, but the praise should be specific. Don't overpraise or list a series of generic attributes, as this will sound insincere. Instead, describe in detail the specific actions or attributes that particularly earned this person the award. Telling an anecdote about this person that illustrates these qualities can be especially effective.

In addition to praising the person receiving the award, you should talk a bit about the award itself. There may be people in the audience who aren't already familiar with it. You might, for example, give a brief history of the award. When was it first given? How many recipients have there been? What is the purpose of the award? What exactly is being rewarded? What does one do to win the award? How many people are considered for it? What determines who the winner will be?

The conclusion of your speech should be the presentation of the award to the recipient. Make a formal statement that includes the name of the award and the name of the winner, such as: "I am now pleased to bring you the winner of the Best Employee Award of 1998, Lisa Stern." Wait for the recipient to come forward, and shake hands and congratulate them when they do. Then turn over the floor to them to make their acceptance speech.

When accepting an award, you should sincerely convey how you feel about receiving this award, as well as how honored and appreciative you are. Do not, however, talk about your worthiness of this award. Whoever presented the award to you will have already done that, and if you speak about your own achievements, you'll sound egotistical. Instead take the time to thank anyone in your life who has helped you in some way to achieve this award, as well as the people conferring it.

It's also in good taste to make some positive comment about your competition. Don't, however, talk about how unworthy you are to receive the award or say someone else really should have gotten it. That might come across as being ungrateful or insincere and will only make the other people feel worse. People in the audience will want to see someone who is happy to receive this award.

You don't need to prepare a long, formal acceptance speech. As long as you share your genuine emotional response at this moment, people in the audience should respond positively to your speech.

GIVING A TOAST

A toast is a type of personal homage that is generally given on milestone occasions. The important factors for giving any personal homage apply here: The toast should be personal and sincere. Your toast doesn't need to be very scripted and can be loosely structured and casual. You should, though, take time to think carefully about what you want to say. Usually you'll be making the toast because you have some kind of relationship with the person being toasted. So speak from the heart about your feelings for the person and share actual stories about him or her. Depending on your personality and the occasion, you might want to include humorous stories or jokes, but be careful not to be offensive.

As casual as a toast can be, it is also somewhat formal in that it should always culminate in the actual toast. Here you ask everyone to join you in raising your glass and toasting the honoree. As you toast, you should try to include some kind of formal remark. Don't just say "cheers" or "bottom's up." While you might simply say, "Here's to _____" and name the honoree(s), the best toasts are more specific and more poetic. A toast is like a blessing that you confer on this person, such as:

> "May the wind always be at your back and the road always rise to meet you."
> "May your love be like your wedding rings—without end—and may we all be present to take part in the joy it brings you."

There are several books available that include sample toasts like these that you can consult to find an appropriate one for you. You can also try to write your own. Phrase it as a comment about what you wish for this person in the future. Write something from the heart and everyone will be moved by it.

RUNNING A PRESS CONFERENCE

A press conference is given to make some big announcement to the media about a newsworthy event, followed by an opportunity for members of the press to ask specific questions about it. It's much like a Q & A session, although with a few important differences.

You should prepare some kind of statement that you plan in advance and set down on paper. Always begin a press conference by reading this piece out loud from start to finish. This will ensure you get the opportunity to convey whatever important piece of information you have to impart without interruption. Start the press conference by telling the people attending that you will first a brief statement and *then* take questions. They'll then know to keep quiet and let you speak.

Unlike at Q & A sessions after speeches or panels, when only some members in the audience raise their hands, at a press conference they will *all* be anxious to ask a question. This can make the situation somewhat chaotic. When calling on someone in the audience, make it very clear exactly whom you are addressing. Either call on a person by name, or point directly at him or her. You won't be able to, nor will you necessarily want to take questions from everyone attending. Try, though, to take questions in a random fashion from people all around the room. That will indicate that you aren't necessarily playing favorites. Avoid taking more than one question from a particular source.

When it comes to responding to these questions, you can follow many of the procedures outlined above for Q & A sessions. Try to anticipate possible questions and formulate responses in advance.

At many press conferences, there may be certain pieces of information you can share with the press, and others that are to remain confidential. Before the press conference, make certain you know exactly what you are allowed to discuss or reveal and what you are to keep confidential. If you cannot or do not want to answer a particular question, simply say that you have no comment or information to share at the present time and then call on someone else. In a regular speech or panel discussion, this kind of response might seem insulting, but in a press conference it's considered entirely appropriate.

Set a time limit for the press conference in advance and announce it at the start. When you near the finish, announce that there's time for one more question. Take that question, respond to it, thank everyone for coming, then exit the room.

SPEAKING ON TELEVISION AND RADIO

There are three main circumstances in which you might be asked to speak on television or the radio: you might be invited to give a prepared statement, to be interviewed, or to participate in a panel or roundtable discussion.

If you are invited to give a prepared statement, find out how much time you have been allotted and make certain you carefully time and edit your statement to fit that time. Usually these statements will be very brief. Make certain you have a strong, memorable opening remark to engage the audience's attention, and an equally strong closing remark that they'll remember. In general, this statement should include sharp and concise sentences as these are easier for an audience to focus on. Don't use long, overly wordy sentences, and keep the language simple and direct. Think of the statement as a series of "sound bites"—short, catchy, sloganlike phrases that are easily remembered and quoted by those in the audience.

If you are reading your statement on television, find out from someone who works on the program if you can use a TelePrompTer or cue cards. A TelePrompTer is like a television screen on which your statement is projected in a long scroll. As you read, the printed words move upward, and you can continue reading along as the next part of your statement appears. The TelePrompTer is usually built right into the television camera, so that as you read your statement, you are looking into the lens, thus appearing on screen as if you are looking directly at the viewers.

If no TelePrompTer is available, you may be able to prepare and use cue cards. Write out your statement on a series of large pieces of cardboard in large block letters that you can read from a distance. Someone will then hold up the cards for you to read from during the broadcast. The cue cards should be situated alongside whatever camera will be focused on you so that in reading the cards you are also directly facing the camera.

If you can't use cue cards or a TelePrompTer, then try to memorize your statement. That way you can give your statement while staring directly at the camera, which will look to the viewers as if you are speaking directly to them rather than staring down at pieces of paper.

When appearing on television, wear solid-colored clothing. Avoid clothing with any kind of patterns, even simple ones, as they don't appear well on television. You should also avoid jewelry and wearing anything with a shine, as the studio lights will reflect off this material creating a glare.

Watch your posture. Make certain you sit up straight and keep your eye focused on the camera. Avoid making broad gestures and blinking too much, as these actions appear overly exaggerated and strange to television viewers. Instead, concentrate on maintaining direct eye contact with the camera, as if this is a single person to whom you are directing your words. Speak slowly and deliberately.

If your appearance is to be an interview or panel discussion, you can use the same strategies outlined earlier for Q & A sessions and panel discussions. You don't, though, need to repeat the questions, as the audience won't have trouble hearing them and you'll only be wasting their time. Try in general, as you would with reading a statement, to keep your comments simple and concise. Come prepared with a few "sound bites" you've already written and then try to weave them into your responses.

When being interviewed or participating in a discussion, you generally don't need to worry about looking at a specific camera. Simply have a conversation with the interviewer or the other panelists; look at them when you speak and direct your remarks to them. The director and camera crew will determine which camera angles to use.

IMPROMPTU SPEECHES

You're attending a panel discussion or meeting, and you've been sitting quietly listening to the various speakers. Suddenly, the chair points at you, introduces you to the audience, and tells everyone that you happen to be somewhat of an expert on this particular subject. Then she asks if you would mind sharing some of your thoughts on the subject with the audience. Yikes! What do you do now?

This is what is known as an impromptu speech—when you are asked to speak before an audience without having been given time to prepare anything in advance. Obviously this kind of speech is going to be challenging as you don't have the opportunity to brainstorm ideas, do research, and plot a clear and effective organization. However, it's not impossible. Here are some tips for giving an impromptu speech that can be just as impressive and effective as a speech written in advance.

1. Anticipate bing asked to speak. Try to be aware of different situations in which you might be asked to say a few words—such as meetings, panel discussions, conventions, or social functions you are attending—and then think a bit about what you *would* say *if* invited to speak. Don't, however, take up too much of your time wondering about this. Most often, you *won't* be asked to speak. But it is worth considering for a few minutes, perhaps while you are getting dressed or driving to the event.

2. Buy yourself some time. In some instances, someone will ask you to speak at a later point during the event. This will give you some time to think about what you want to say. However, if you are asked to begin speaking immediately, you can still try to stall for a bit of time. Take your time approaching the lectern. Take a long pause before you begin. Take a drink of water. If someone has posed a question to you, repeat it. Or start speaking with some very general remarks. Do whatever you can to give yourself a moment to think.

3. Decide on a main idea and key points—and stick to them. As with a regular speech, an effective impromptu speech should focus on one main idea that you particularly want to communicate to the audience. Decide quickly for yourself what that idea is as well as the other key points you'd like to make. Then stick to them. Don't change the direction of your speech midway, and don't jump around from one idea to another or take numerous digressions. Decide on the focus for your speech and stick to it.

4. Follow the three-part structure. As you speak, follow the same three-part structure we discussed in part one of the book: Include an opening with a hook, a body, and a concluding statement.

As far as selecting a hook, you might want to memorize several quotations that you particularly like and that have multiple applications. Whenever you are asked to give an impromptu speech, you can then select one of these quotations and use it as an opening hook. You'll then just need to improvise some way to connect it to the rest of your speech.

For the body, you should also decide on some basic organization as we discussed in Chapter 4. You might, for example, decide to tell a story in chronological order. Listing a variety of points by number is a particularly easy way to organize an impromptu speech that doesn't require a great deal of thought or preparation. Simply tell the audience you have three things you'd like to tell them about or three points you'd like to make, and then go ahead and discuss those three items.

5. Make no apologies. When you begin speaking, do not apologize to the audience that you haven't prepared something to say. If you've just been invited to speak in front of them, they'll understand that this is an impromptu speech and won't be expecting anything polished. Throughout the speech, speak with confidence and authority, without apologizing or bemoaning your lack of preparation. Don't ever undercut your speech by saying things like "I didn't mean to say that," or "that's not what I really meant to discuss." By making these kinds of apologizes, you detract from the power of what you are saying; people in the audience will think it's not all that important. Instead, if you speak with confidence and even enthusiasm, it will sound like you do care about what your are saying, making a very positive impression on the audience.

6. Keep it short and slow. No one expects an impromptu speech to be long, so don't feel compelled to give a keynote address. By keeping it short, you can keep it much more focused and organized. The opening hook and concluding statement only need to be a line or two; the body only needs to address a few key points. As you speak, talk at a very slow pace. This will give you more opportunity to think about what you will say next before you go ahead and say it. Don't say "um" and "er" while trying to think about what to say next. Just pause, think, and then being speaking. Those pauses actually won't seem all that obvious or disruptive to the audience. You'll just sound like a thoughtful professional speaker who speaks slowly, forcefully, and deliberately.

7. Finish off with a real concluding statement. The concluding remark should be some kind of memorable statement that brings your speech to a definite close. As with the hook, you might again use some quotation you've already memorized. Just make certain you come to a firm conclusion. Speakers sometimes make the mistake of thinking they should just keep talking until they run out of things to say about the topic. The speech then rambles on and then peters out undramatically. Instead, you should stick to a few key points and then end with a statement that sounds like a definite conclusion.

Part III:

Sample Speeches

A WORD ON THE SAMPLE SPEECHES

In this third section, you'll find a variety of sample speeches for different occasions. These speeches are meant to serve as models for how you might clearly and effectively organize and present ideas and information in speeches with specific purposes. You'll find that, as they were written for the sake of demonstration, most of them are somewhat generic and relatively short. When writing your own speeches, you usually will want to make them longer and include more details and specific information related to your own particular aim, audience, occasion, and venue. However, you can certainly use the speeches here to provide you with ideas and examples.

BOOSTING MORALE

The poet Theodore Roethke once said, "In a dark time, the eye begins to see." And in the wake of these recent layoffs, in this dark time of tremendous insecurity and uncertainty, it is imperative that we maintain a clear vision—both of the way things are now and of the way they will be.

It probably comes as a surprise to no one that after our merger with Calco Pharmaceutical and the consequential layoffs, I have called everyone together. I am not going to pull any punches in this discussion. You are my staff, and I want to be frank with you. I want to tell you what I know about the immediate future of this company. I want to empower you with these facts. I want to create an atmosphere of security, understandably no easy task when some of our coworkers have just been downsized. But we now need to move forward to ensure our own jobs. And I believe together we can do this. Today, I'm going to share with you the three-step plan that is going to take this company into its next phase of existence.

Let me first say, though, that no more layoffs are in the immediate future. If you are sitting in this meeting listening to me, you do have job security. Please take that in. This company needs you. All of your jobs are essential. This is a fact.

Now for our three-step plan for a better, more lucrative future: merging, identifying, and modifying. Step One: Merging. Change is never easy. Transition is often uncomfortable. But the outcome can reap tremendous benefits for all. The merging phase of the three-step plan is going to be the hardest. The way we are used to doing our work is going to be questioned. Our operations and methods will be closely scrutinized. It is enough to make the most secure worker feel a little shaky. But, hear me, this is just part of the process. Nothing about this phase is personal. We are not looking to cut back any more. We are looking to move forward.

You will not be alone during this phase of our plan. This is the most important thing for you to remember. I have an open door. If you need help, please come to me. If you need reassurance and guidance, please come to me. If you just need someone to hear your frustration with this process, please come to me. I am not just paying lip service. During this first phase, my sole job is to be there for you and to make this difficult transition easier for you. Your job during this first phase is to become more aware. Pay attention to what is going on; make observations about what is working and what is superfluous. Think about the positive changes you'd like to see here. Keep notes. The more you notice, the more you can participate in the exciting changes taking place.

Awareness leads us into step two of our plan, identifying. We need now to identify changes we need to make; we also need to identify what already works. Your notes and observations from phase one are critical in phase two. If you're happy here, your comments can help indicate what we need to continue doing to keep you happy; if you are unhappy with what you see going on, they can be used to make changes. But, if your voice isn't heard, you can't be part of the solution. Phase two gives you a real opportunity to create a more idealized work environment. I am not just asking to hear the voices of department heads. I want to hear everyone's opinions—executives, assistants, associates, and staff. During phase two, everyone's opinion carries equal weight. We cannot correct problems we don't know about. I cannot urge you enough to speak out. Please, take advantage of your power.

After we have merged and identified our strengths and weaknesses, we will be ready to move onto phase three, the modification stage. This is the point in our process where we will put your feedback into action. After the corporate department receives your input and analyzes it, we will work on the necessary retooling and revamping to take our company into the twenty-first century.

In summation, what may seem like a dark time of uncertainty to you right now, actually provides an opportunity, as Roethke observed, to see more clearly than ever. Open your eyes. Take notice. Make suggestions. Help us to notice, to identify, and to modify. And if you do, I promise you that you'll find the future looking brighter than ever.

NEW BUSINESS PITCH

It's Generation X versus the Baby Boomers! Look in the advertising and marketing trade papers, and that's all you'll read about. Or just look around you; it seems as if every ad campaign these days is aimed at today's hip youth culture, or at more affluent urban professionals. That's because after spending millions on marketing studies and focus groups, businesses everywhere have decided that targeting one of these two lucrative markets will yield them the highest sales. It's impossible to target everyone, and a specialized ad campaign aimed at a very clearly defined audience is the way to go. Or so the conventional thinking would indicate.

As you've announced your decision to switch ad agencies, I'm betting more than one agency has come to you proclaiming its success in advertising to one of those two core markets. I'm here, though, to tell you it doesn't need to be an either/or situation. What if you could target Generation X *and* the Baby Boomers? And what if you could do it without having to spend more on your advertising budget? Wouldn't your sales then be twice as high?

What the Devon Agency can offer you that you'll find nowhere else is a creative staff that knows both today's youth culture and the baby boomer generation inside and out. That's because we've structured our company in a way that uniquely combines younger and more mature sensibilities. Our creative department consists of several teams, each one pairing older, more experienced art directors and copywriters who have been selling to the Boomer market for the past ten years with younger talents who bring their fresh perspectives and knowledge of today's youth market. We don't play to one market or the other; we play to both. And we're able to do it because our staff comes from both those core demographic groups.

Let me show you some of our exciting work. [SHOW SERIES OF SLIDES OF MAGAZINE ADS.] This is a series of magazine ads we created for Fashion Attic. You can see how we drew upon a range of today's hottest up-and-coming young start, and paired them up with the Oscar winning actors and actresses who are the kings and queens of Hollywood's old guard. Now let me show you how we expanded on that campaign in our television spots [SHOW REEL OF COMMERCIAL CLIPS.] Our account executives were careful to place these ads in a range of media outlets, from TV shows popular with the twenty-one and under set, to more affluent, business-oriented publications.

What did this new campaign mean for Fashion Attic? I'll show you. [PUT CHART ON EASEL.] This chart documents Fashion Attic's sales before and after our campaign. You can see that after the initial launch in the magazines, sales rose 22 percent. And after the commercial spots started running, they rose another staggering 15 percent.

How would you like to see that same kind of increase in sales here at Close Clothes? You've done a remarkable job of making your Casual Khaki pants a fashion staple of the affluent twenty-five to forty year-old set. But why stop there? Why not target those teenagers and college kids? The right campaign, aimed at a broader market, could double your potential sales.

Our work for Fashion Attic that I just showed you has proven what many claim to be impossible: it *is* possible to market to Generation X *and* the Baby Boomers with one campaign. It's possible, but how many agencies are doing it? How many agencies *can* do it? Only the Devon Agency has the kind of diverse mixture of talents—and daring imagination—to make these campaigns work. Let the Devon Agency put those talents to work for you.

PRESENTING AN AWARD

One of the most rewarding components of my job is getting to reward others. And no award gives me greater pleasure to bestow than Employee of the Month. Often the only reward for hard work is the quiet satisfaction of seeing a job well done. And while this pride is meaningful, it is important to the company that we take time to shine a spotlight on individual players on our team.

As you know, since we began awarding an Employee of the Month back in June 1995, we have often lauded employees whose contributions are obvious, such as winning a new client or creating a new campaign. It's important, though, that we take equal pride in those workers whose skillful and steadfast work is an integral part of this company's overall success. For this month's award, the awards committee and myself decided to reward just such a devoted worker—and we knew almost immediately who was most deserving of it. It is with great pride that I bestow this month's Employee of the Month award to Christopher Paceyak.

Christopher is the embodiment of a true company man. His dedication to this company comes through in his every action, from the extra hours he often devotes to his job to his enthusiastic coaching of our softball team. His can-do attitude has been the driving force behind many an outstanding project, which he oversees from start to finish with an eye on perfection. His quiet confidence in times of crisis frequently has a calming effect on even his most stressed-out coworkers, and his morale and good humor have proven downright infectious. Christopher knows that in order for him to look good at his job, it behooves him to have the whole department look good. His colleagues have marveled at how he always knows when someone needs a helping hand and then doesn't bat an eye about offering his services.

In today's often impersonal work world, Christopher always makes sure he is accessible. Our clients often ask for him by name, and his friendly attitude never fails in setting them at ease. I'll never forget the time I went to pitch a new client—the Allenberg Theatre—and at the start of our meeting, they asked me if Christopher Paceyak would be available to work on their account! They'd heard about his wonderful work through our other clients.

Woody Allen once remarked that 80 percent of success is showing up. Christopher has shown that not to be true. It's not just showing up that makes him such an inspiration—although he has maintained a stellar attendance record throughout his employment here—it's the warmth, dedication, and energy he brings with him into this office each and every day that have made all of us a little bit happier to be here. Christopher, it is with great delight that I present you with December's Employee of the Month plaque. We here at Ticketflash would also like to give you a gift certificate for a dinner for four at your favorite local restaurant. Enjoy. Thank you for your devotion. And, Christopher, keep up the great work.

RECEIVING AN AWARD

Sophocles once said, "Look and you will find it—what is unsought will go undetected." It was this philosophy that led me to this company. When I graduated from college ten years ago, I had a definite image in mind of the kind of place where I wanted to work, and I set out to find it. I was looking for a company with the potential to grow, and that I could grow with. I was looking for a nurturing boss who could teach me through example and experience. I was looking for coworkers I could depend on and also consider friends. I was looking for an environment where I could feel free to think creatively and, best of all possible worlds, even be rewarded for it. I knew it was a tall order, but I was determined that if such a company existed, I would find it. I even turned down a few offers because they just didn't seem right. But when I stepped through the doors at Ticketflash, it did seem to have it all. Ten years later, I'm happy to say that initial search yielded exactly what I'd been seeking—and more.

I don't know many people who are still excited, ten years down the line, to get out of bed to go to work. But I am. And to receive an award for something I love doing is a true gift for which I am grateful.

When I found out that I was being given this award, it gave me time to reflect on the period of time I have spent at Ticketflash. I will never forget the first major account I ran, the Second Avenue

Theater. The theater director was a real character, and I worked day and night trying to please him. As our first season working with them came to a close, I went out with some coworkers to celebrate making it through without a major mishap. Wouldn't you know, though, that I got a call from the director that very night? It seemed that a batch of tickets we'd ordered for them had been printed entirely in purple. Well, I thought he was going to flip his lid. I also thought that would put a fast end to my employment here. But I got the surprise of my life when he then told me how he always hated the old tickets and that purple was his favorite color. So I learned a valuable lesson. Success has a lot to do with hard work, time, and effort, but sometimes luck plays a part in it too. And I've been very lucky.

I've been lucky to work with such incredible people whom I admire and love. Marlon, thank you for the gracious and moving presentation. This is overwhelming. I have worked under you for my entire tenure here. I have learned immeasurable business savvy from you. In my estimation, this award is as much yours as it is mine. I would not be accepting an award of excellence without the wisdom and confidence you have imparted to me. Thank you.

Josh, Katherine, and Kyle, you are the working definition of a dream team. Many people might not think of marketing as a creative field. But with our group, I feel like the Beatles must have felt when they would create a hit song. All elements come together in perfect harmony. And, Josh, I'm not even going to mention the fact that you led the company softball team to the league championships two years in a row! I truly couldn't dream of three more upstanding and fine people I would rather spend such a large chunk of my life with. Thank you. Thank you. Thank you.

I've also been lucky, throughout the years, to have so many wonderful clients whom I've been honored to work with, many of whom, I'm touched to see, are here tonight. Clients with whom I feel so very proud to be associated. Clients I am glad to call friends.

I want to wrap up by once again thanking everyone for giving me this beautiful night, this wonderful award. Your caring guidance, your warm camaraderie, your business! Thank you for giving me a glorious memory of a very proud and happy time in my life, a memory I am sure to reflect upon for years to come. I am truly honored to receive your award of excellence.

HONORING A RETIRING EMPLOYEE

Somerset Maugham once said, "It's a funny thing about life; if you refuse to accept anything but the best, you very often get it." As the head of this company, I have tried to live by this motto, always expecting the best from myself and from everyone who works here. Over the years, some have not seen the value of this thinking and left. Others did value it and left anyway. And then there's Charlie Ryan, who stayed. Charlie stayed for thirty-five years! And each and every day he's been here, he's not only strived to do his best, but inspired everyone around him, myself included, to do so as well.

Charlie, nobody deserves to take it easy more than you do. In your thirty-five years here, you have put so much into this company that it's impossible to imagine what it would have been like had you never walked through our doors. And now, it's impossible to imagine Clearview Industries without your commitment, your energy, your passion. I have never lost a night's sleep over the fate of this company knowing you were around. Charlie, you have been a rock for me and for all of us.

You've been a shining example to so many people here. So many people approached me this week to share a story about you and talk about how much they will miss you. As a tribute to you, I'd like to single a few of them out and share with all of you what they told me about how much Charlie has meant to them.

First, I'd like to ask Brad Green to stand up. Brad came to Clearview fresh from Indiana University. His only practical work experience was a part-time cold call sales job for Mertin Lyle.

Charlie, you took Brad under your wing and taught him how to sell. You shared your own work ethic and experience with him, telling him stories of the good old days. And Brad tells me that you made him lists of books to read—philosophy books, business books, even a book of poetry—books that you told Brad give a business executive his backbone. You took Brad to your business meetings. Introduced him to your clients. Treated him with respect. Treated him as an equal. You gave Brad the room to make mistakes, room to have triumphs. Charlie, you gave Brad the tools that helped him earn this company over two million dollars last year.

Another person whose life has been forever altered for having known you is Dolores Klein. Dolores, please stand up. Dolores has done everything from photocopying and faxing Charlie's documents to giving a speech for Charlie when he had laryngitis! Needless to say, the two of them have been quite a team for over twenty years. When Dolores' dear husband Alex passed away eight years ago with no life insurance, Charlie did more than pay a condolence call. Charlie established a trust fund for Dolores' daughter Shelley. Shelley is now in her third year at Fordham University. Shelley is the first person to go to college in Dolores' family, and she will always have you to thank for such a generous and selfless gift.

I know Brad and Dolores are going to miss you, Charlie. We all are. You better not get so good at golf that you don't let me beat you at least every once in a while! I know that you and Susan are excited to move into your condo in Arizona. I know you are excited to be close to your five beautiful grandchildren. I know that you are excited to write that great American novel you are always going on about. I know you are excited to start this new phase of your life.

I am excited for you. But, Charlie, I just want you to know that this company will never be the same without you. I believe I will miss you and think of you every day I continue to run this place. Thank you, Charlie. Thank you for your service. Thank you for being such an inspiration. And, Charlie, thank you for being a friend. Charlie, all of us here wish you all the health, love, and happiness you so much deserve.

ADDRESS TO STOCKHOLDERS

We all know that stockholder's meetings can be dreadfully dull. But you can breathe easy. That's not going to be the case here. As we begin our first stockholder meeting here at Flowers Plus, I'm going to set a precedent and start a new yearly tradition. The precedent is that our meeting will be brief and to the point—providing you with all the information you need to know clearly, quickly, and efficiently. And the tradition? I'll get to that later.

Without further adieu, let's look at the facts. If you will consult the hand-outs we have prepared for you and turn to page three, you will see that in our first quarter, Flowers Plus had a 17 percent increase in profits. As this is our maiden voyage, we are thrilled with this progress. The second quarter projections look even rosier. Okay, I promise, no more flower puns!

We plan to reinvest our profits from quarter one, but we need to decide where and how. Our market research indicates that the money might best be invested into our Internet division. Our Internet division netted the company over $100,000 in its first quarter, and the World Wide Web shows no signs of slowing down. There is huge growth potential here. After much analysis, we believe that our sales will increase directly in proportion to our investments in this area. But we need to take a vote on this matter. Once you have reviewed the collateral material we have provided you with, please fill out the ballot at the back of the packet indicating your support of or opposition to this reinvestment.

Last on our agenda today is a review of Flowers Plus's retail division. Our retail stores are covering their own costs and should start to pull a profit starting next quarter. However, our flower stands made a profit right out of the gate. We propose to take the profits from the stands and use them for in-store promotions at our retail outlets. As you already know, Flowers Plus has primarily marketed itself with a strong commitment to teaching the consumer to have a green thumb. We can expand on this image by giving in-store seminars. This is a relatively inexpensive way to create goodwill and generate new business and hopefully even media buzz all at once. You'll find a detailed proposal in your packet regarding this exciting possibility. You can review it and we'll open it up to discussion at our next quarterly meeting.

To sum up: In our first quarter, we have made more of a profit than our projections indicated. We now want to reinvest in our Internet division and need your vote. And we want to take the excess profits from our stands and funnel the money into retail promotions.

Now, for starting that tradition that I referred to earlier. We'd like to invite you back to our corporate garden where we are going to plant flowers. We hope to end every stockholder's meeting with this activity. To us, it's a symbol of how working together, we can all take a part in the growth of our company.

ANALYZING A PROBLEM/PROPOSING A SOLUTION

Albert Einstein once said, "In the middle of difficulty lies opportunity." And right now, the Plunkett Corporation has its difficulty, namely our sharp decline in sales. But rather than becoming panicked by this downturn, I'd like to take Mr. Einstein's advice. After all, he was a pretty smart man. And I am confident that we do have an opportunity here. Not only can we solve our problems and reverse this decline, but in so doing, we can also make changes that will eventually raise our profits higher than ever. I'll tell you exactly how we can do that in a moment.

But before I can share with you my program for combating our problems, it's important that you first understand them. As you know, I have hired an independent consulting firm to come in and help us analyze this situation. After a three-week period in which they've interviewed and observed us carefully, they have identified three major factors behind Plunkett Corporation's drop in sales that I want to now share with you.

One, we are losing our retailers. Several key retailers have stopped ordering from us entirely, and those that we still have dealings with have been ordering from us far less frequently. Speaking with representatives from these retailers, our consultants heard complaints about the lack of personal contact they receive from us and what they perceive as a decline in service. Our retailers have become frustrated with dealing with our sales reps via telephone and fax, and complain of the difficulty they've had getting responses to their questions and problems. As a result, many of them have turned to other companies with better service.

Two, we are losing consumers. At one time, our marketing and advertising worked for us, but it has become terribly outdated. We've typically geared ourselves to the twenty- to thirty-year-old demographic group. But as they've aged, they've stopped using our products, and we've failed to create new marketing and advertising to appeals to today's youth market. Simply put, we're no longer reaching the people we need to.

And three, we are losing money, money that we shouldn't be losing. The consulting team has prepared a listing of all of our unnecessary expenditures that I am now making available to you. Individual items on this list cost as little as pennies and nickels a day, which is why we often don't give them serious consideration. But when added together, they cost us an astonishing $100,000 in unnecessary spending each month!

So, thanks to our consultants, we now know the three factors behind our declining sales: losing our retailers through poor service, our consumers through outdated marketing and advertising, and our money through wasteful and unnecessary expenditures. That's the bad news. The good news is that having identified the problems we have now come up with solutions.

First, based on the listing of expenditures provided by our consultants, I am trimming the fat here, effective immediately. I am passing out to each of you the new, far more modest monthly budgets for each department. By cutting those pennies and nickels spent each day on the unnecessaries you'll find you still have plenty of money for your operating costs.

Second, I am going to take the money cut from those budgets to help us foster better relations with our retailers and customers. To begin with, I am authorizing more on-site sales visits within the tri-state area. Within the week, I want every member of the sales staff to create a sales call itinerary for themselves and submit it to me. I am also instituting a new bonus system; for each client who you get and hold onto for the year, you'll receive an additional $500 at year's end. Do what you need to keep those clients and keep them happy.

Third, I want us to work closely with marketing to revamp and add to our marketing materials. For one thing, we need to present the most up-to-date sales brochures as possible. Perception is everything and we need to appear as current as we actually are. We cannot afford to look out of date. Technology is moving so fast that what was current even months ago is now obsolete. We need to stay on top of the trends. I'm also hiring a new advertising agency and increasing our advertising budget. We're going to create new, more aggressive campaigns and target them to a broader market.

This is the program I've developed along with our consultants. But I can only put the initial steps in place; you're the ones who have got to make them work. If you succeed, though—and I am certain you will—not only will this time of difficulty be at an end, but we just might be entering a time of our greatest prosperity, and we'll all be able to take part in the benefits. When next we meet, rather than looking at our failures and difficulties, let's be in a position to celebrate our profits and triumphs.

DEDICATING A NEW FACILITY

St. Bart's Hospital is a Mayfield institution. It has been in existence for over seventy years, and as our community has grown, so has this important facility. The babies born in Mayfield are born at St. Bart's, and the lives saved in Mayfield are saved at St. Bart's. Another Mayfield institution is the Sylvester family. For three generations this family has been a very important part of this community. From Jim Sylvester's service as the high school principal to Lucy Sylvester's successful tenure as our mayor, this family has given so much to their home town.

Five years ago, the St. Bart's development office received a mixed blessing. We were saddened by the passing of beloved Agnes Sylvester, the matriarch of the Sylvester family. Yet we were surprised and very grateful to learn that in her will, Mrs. Sylvester donated two hundred thousand dollars to St. Bart's to break ground on a new children's wing.

Caring for children was an issue near and dear to Mrs. Sylvester's heart, as it is to the staff at St. Bart's. That is why today we are proud to have the surviving members of the Sylvester family on hand for the groundbreaking and ribbon-cutting ceremony for the new Agnes Sylvester Wing for Children at the St. Bart's Hospital. Children represent our future. As we remember the passing of Agnes Sylvester, let us take comfort in the thought of the many children who will be cared for and even saved at this new facility. In this way, her memory will truly live on.

And now, without further ado, I invite Agnes Sylvester's eldest son, Lee, to please cut the ribbon so that construction may begin on what will be his family's newest contribution to Mayfield.

GIVING A DEMONSTRATION

I have in my hand a stack of phone message pads. And I'm now going to throw them in the trash. Because with our new voice mail system, they're no longer necessary. Yes, I know you're all a little concerned about having to learn how to use this new voice mail system. But consider this. The days of writing out messages by hand—and all the tedium and miscommunication that went with it—are now over and done with. I can honestly say that within a week, you will be operating the Vspeak 2000 like old pros—and you'll see just how much better this system is than the old way.

It's also not nearly as hard to use as you might think. I'm going to take you step by step through the new system. Feel free to take notes if you like, although I will also be providing you with an operations manual that describes everything I'll be showing you. We'll be looking at the three most important facets of this new system: First we are going to discuss call transfers; we will then move onto the voice mail set up; and finally, voice mail retrieval.

Let's start with call transferring. Suppose I answer a call that is actually for Larry Wilkes and I need to transfer it to him. You'll see on these charts that I've distributed that you have all been assigned extension numbers. So when I get the call, I just need to check the extension chart and see that Larry's extension is 220. To transfer this call to him, I first hit the transfer button [SHOW BUTTON ON SAMPLE PHONE], located at the bottom right hand corner of the phone unit. Next, I dial Larry's extension and then I hang up. Let me show you. [DEMONSTRATE TRANS-FER]. It's that simple.

I do not, I repeat, I do not hit the hold button during this trans-fer. It's a common urge that people have to put someone on hold before they transfer a call. If you do hit the hold button, the call will not transfer. But don't worry if you make a mistake and hit the hold button anyway. The worst thing that would happen is that your caller will sit on hold for a minute and then your line will ring again. It's very easy. All you need to remember to transfer a call is transfer-extension-transfer.

Let's say Larry Wilkes is not at his desk or he's on an another line and can't get off to answer the other ringing line. The call will then go into voice mail. After five rings, the Vspeak 2000 automatically puts a call into voice mail. What the caller will hear first is a generic greeting. Let's try calling Larry's line right now and hear it. [DEMONSTRATE CALL ON SPEAKERPHONE]. What you just heard was the generic greeting already pro-grammed into the system. Now, if this message is satisfactory to you, you can simply leave it on your phone. However, many peo-ple choose to personalize their outgoing voice mail message. Larry, why don't you come up here and I will guide you through recording your own personal voice mail message? Everyone else can do this when they go back to their own desks at the end of the demonstration. [WAIT FOR LARRY TO COME UP.]

All right, Larry. You can either compose your own message, or use the standard script we've provided. You are about to be recorded; are you nervous Larry? Take a deep breath and don't worry about it. You can record your message as many times as you want until you are satisfied. First hit the feature button and then 435. You will then be prompted through the process. I'll put it on speakerphone for you all to hear. You can also follow the instructions in your instruction manual. [HAVE LARRY RECORD HIS MESSAGE/EVERYONE LISTENS ON SPEAKERPHONE]. Okay, now that the message is recorded, you just need to hit feature *** to save it. So, to review: to record a personalized voice mail message, hit feature 435, follow the recorded instructions, and then to save your greeting, hit feature ***.

You can rerecord your personalized messages whenever you like. For example, if you are going away on vacation, you can rerecord your message to tell your callers that you will be out of the office for a week and to dial your assistant's extension for help. Or you can give an alternative phone number at which you can be reached.

The final process I want to review with you today is voice mail retrieval. There are two ways that you can retrieve voice mail. One way is internally, the other is externally. Internally means that you retrieve your messages from somewhere in your office. If you are sitting at your own extension, for example, you can simply hit the voice mail button and punch in your code, and your messages will then play back. Everyone has a code that must be entered to get messages off voice mail, so you don't have to worry about anyone hearing something meant only for you. To receive your secret code, hit feature 456 and let the prompt guide you. If you are at another extension in the office, you simply hit feature 999 and you will be prompted to enter your extension and then your code and then you can receive your messages. Larry, why don't you retrieve messages from my voice mail? [DEMONSTRATE RETRIEVAL OF MESSAGES FROM VOICE MAIL].

Finally, if you are calling from outside the office, you can dial the main number and ask the receptionist to put you through to your own extension. Once connected to your extension, hit feature 227 and you will be prompted to give your password or code and then you can retrieve your messages. If you are calling during nonbusiness hours, you will be placed into the general voice mail mailbox. You then hit the # key and then feature 724. The prompt will then ask you for your extension. After you punch in your extension, hit the # key again. This will take you to the prompt that asks for your personal code. And that's it; you can retrieve your messages.

I don't want to overload you with too much information today. So, why doesn't everybody go back to his or her desk and record messages. I will be back next week to go through some more features of the Vspeak 2000. I guarantee that by then, you'll be telling me you don't know what you did without voice mail for so long.

RUNNING A MEETING

We've all heard the saying that "talk is cheap." I'm not so certain I agree with that. One thing I've seen in our monthly staff meetings is just how valuable talking can be. The discussions we've had here have led to important policy changes that have resulted in a number of noticeable improvements in this company. So I firmly believe that talk is definitely not cheap; in fact, I think it is crucial to our continued success.

However, I have been thinking about another factor that is perhaps even more valuable than talking, a skill that we've unfortunately overlooked too often. And that's listening. All of us here are quite skilled orators. We know how to make our points clearly, convincingly, and eloquently. But how many of us are skilled listeners? More and more I'm convinced that active listening—making a concentrated effort to really listen to one another—is the only way we can get an accurate picture of what's happening in this company. It's also the best way for us all to work toward solving problems and to generate great new ideas.

So I've decided to make listening the focus of today's meeting; as I see it, listening, in some way or other, informs our agenda today in three important ways.

First, I've personally been doing a great deal of listening myself lately. I've spent the last two weeks visiting each and every department in our company, making a it my main goal to listen to what our employees have to say. Based on what I heard, I have identified four issues that appear to be most in need of immediate consideration: one, the new computer system; two, the overtime hours issue; three, the development of the company Web site; and four, the loss of the D&R account.

Second, I want you to listen to each other in today's meeting as carefully as I have listened to all of you in the past two weeks. To that end, I have asked each department head to prepare a brief report that touches on the issues I just listed. While each department head reads that report today, make it your sole aim to listen. Really listen. Don't take notes. Don't make comments. Don't even ask questions. Just listen.

Third, when each department head is finished speaking, when we've all listened to what he or she has to say, then there will be time for talk. We can open the floor for questions and for open discussion. However, again, I'd ask that you all concentrate on those listening skills. Rather than just making a comment, or offering an opinion, listen to what the person before you has said. See if you can build on that topic and somehow incorporate it into your own statement. This will insure that we're all actively listening to one another.

I think we'll find these efforts at active listening make the meeting much more productive. Feel free, afterwards, to let me know what you think. I can guarantee, I'll listen to whatever you have to say.

Now, time for us to listen to our first speaker: Carol Jacobson from Financing. Go ahead, Carol, the floor is yours . . .

GIVING A WEDDING TOAST

When David asked me to be his best man, I have to admit I felt nervous at the thought of giving this toast. It made me nervous because I realized I'd have to somehow pick from the thousands of embarrassing stories involving David's bizarre dating experiences that I know. I thought I might tell you about the time he managed to break his nose while out on a blind date. I also thought I could tell you about the date who managed to steal David's wallet during their romantic dinner. But then I figured, no. It's his wedding, so I'll give the guy a break. Instead of embarrassing him, I'll tell a story about myself. It just so happens to be the story of how I met Lisa, now Mrs. David Bernstein, for the first time.

I'd been hearing David describe this fantastic new woman in his life for weeks. Based on everything he told me about Lisa and her background, I had a picture of her in my mind as being pretty high class and stylish, on par with say Grace Kelly or Audrey Hepburn. So you can imagine how panicked I was when, one Saturday night, minutes after I'd come in from a run, David buzzed my apartment to tell me that he and Lisa were downstairs and wanted to come up.

I had been working all week on a nightmarish project that kept me at the office until late hours. To call my apartment a sty at that point is probably an insult to pigs. And this was the time David chose to introduce me to his Grace Kelly. So I did what any guy in my position would do—I tried to hide the mess; you know, frantically shoving the pizza boxes under the coach, putting dirty dishes back in cabinets, stuff like that. I didn't have time, though, to change out of my sweaty workout clothes I was still wearing after my run.

Well, David and Lisa come in, and of course Lisa couldn't be any nicer. After kissing me hello, she went to the fridge, helped herself to a beer, and threw herself down on the couch to relax. Within about five minutes, after we'd compared notes about our favorite TV shows and movies, I felt like I'd known her as long as I did David. And I've only felt even closer to her ever since.

As many of you probably know, when your best friend gets married, it can be a wonderful, happy occasion. But I also hope you know, like I do, the special joy you get when your best friend marries someone you can consider a friend. And so, I'd like you all to lift up your glasses to toast the happy couple with me.

To David and Lisa, may your love, like your wedding rings, be without end. And may all of us be there to share in the joy it brings you.

WELCOME TO COMPANY OUTING

Ever since I saw the movie *The Shining,* I've been pretty sensitive to the dangers of overwork. You probably know the scene I'm thinking of. Shelley Duvall comes to check up on her husband Jack Nicholson's progress on the novel he's been slaving away at, and finds he's written over and over, "All work and no play makes Jack a dull boy." That's right before he goes bonkers and tries to kill her with an axe. Since I've lately been detecting that same "Jack-like" glint in some of your eyes, especially the folks over in marketing, I think our company outing couldn't come at a better time.

All kidding aside, we've all been working incredibly hard the past few months. Taking on that massive D&R account meant our workload increased by more than 30 percent. For most of you, it meant long hours. It meant late nights. And it meant plenty of stress. But everyone at Jones & Robertson rose to the challenge. And as a result of all that extra effort, I'm proud to announce that we had our most successful quarter ever.

And that's something worth celebrating with a day off. So we've rented this fabulous club for your exclusive use for the entire day. I hope you'll find something to do you enjoy. Play tennis or golf, take a dip in the pool, or enjoy a steam in the sauna. Later on, we'll have a terrific barbecue out on the lake. Just one thing: you are officially forbidden to discuss anything at all having to do with D&R, the office, or work! Talking about work can make Jack a dull boy too! Today is about fun. Today is about rest and relaxation. You've had your weeks of "all work," now it's time to play.

PRESS CONFERENCE ANNOUNCEMENT

Thank you all for coming on such short notice. Those of you who don't know me, I'm Jacqueline Bruckner, vice president of public relations for Netsurf Enterprises. Beside me is William Berg, head of press relations for Global Entertainment.

First I'll read a brief statement, and then both Mr. Berg and myself will be available to answer your questions.

After six months of negotiation talks, the boards of directors of Netsurf and Global Entertainment have finalized arrangements for a merger between the two companies to go into effect on January 1 of next year. The new company will be called Global Netsurf, and the merger will make it the largest new media production company in existence. Bringing together the technology developed by Netsurf with the resources of Global Entertainment, Global Netsurf will be able to provide computer uses with an unprecedented number of entertainment resources made available exclusively over the Internet.

Laura Smith, former president of Netsurf, will serve as the CEO of the new company. Roger Atkins, former head of Global Entertainment, will serve as president of production. The corporate headquarters of Global Netsurf will remain in New York, while the product development and production facilities will move to a new location to be determined. At this time, there are no plans to layoff any employees from either company.

Now, Mr. Berg and myself are happy to take some of your questions. I should first explain, though, that at this time, we are only authorized to answer questions having to do with the structure of and future agenda for the new company, and how the merger will affect consumers, employees, and stockholders. We cannot at this time disclose any specific terms of the merger agreement. However, Ms. Smith and Mr. Atkins will both be available to answer questions at a future press conference.

WELCOMING A NEW EMPLOYEE

My grandmother, who is without a doubt the wisest person I know, has a simple yet tremendously insightful philosophy about cooking. She says, when it comes to cooking, "if you put in good, you get good." And she's right. She always prepares meals using the freshest, most tasty, most high quality ingredients; and by putting those fine ingredients into her cooking, whatever she makes always comes out superb.

As the director of human resources for Aztec, Inc., I've found myself using my grandmother's philosophy as a guidepost for hiring all new employees. Like my grandmother and her faith in good ingredients, I've believed that, by "putting good" into this company, "good" will result. So I've made a commitment to seeking out only the best, most accomplished and skilled people to come be a part of Aztec, Inc. And the results of those hiring practices are evident in this company's outstanding achievements, that only seem to increase with each talented new person who joins us.

Today, we welcome a new ingredient to our extraordinary company mix, someone who has already proven herself to be a genius at what she does. Andrea Gold, who joins us today as a vice president of marketing, comes to us from Zip Four Communications, where she worked in the marketing department for the past eight years. In addition to working on an impressive list of high-profile accounts that includes Cryon Comm, Bengal, and Genie.com, Andrea was the genius behind the "Synergy"

campaign, which set new industry standards in computer market-
ing strategies. That campaign also earned Andrea 1998's
"Marketing Mind" of the Year Award from the American
Association of Communications and Marketing Professionals.

Yes, there's no question that, in the world of marketing,
Andrea is one of the best there is working today, and we are very
lucky to have her. I'm certain that she'll be "putting good" into
our company, and we'll all benefit from her contribution in the
days to come.

I hope in the next few days, you'll take the time to introduce
yourselves to Andrea and to make her feel welcome. Help her to
blend in and become a part of this special, talented mix we are so
fortunate to have here at Aztec.

FAREWELL TO A DEPARTING EMPLOYEE

Marcus Aurelius Antoninus, a Roman emperor and philosopher,
once offered these wise words: "Loss is nothing else but change,
and change is Nature's delight." In thinking about how I might
offer a fond farewell to Susan Atkinson, I had cause to think
about those words. While we are sad to lose Susan, her departure
from here is certain to be the delight, if not of Nature Herself,
then certainly of all who are fortunate to work with her in the
future.

Susan first came to Lerner, Lerner and Kaye in 1990, as a first
year associate who had just graduated with distinction from New
York University Law School. We knew she was special right from
day one, when she was thrust into the morass of the Ryan vs.
Ryan case, and proved herself much more than capable; her long
hours, her careful research, and her instrumental input all played
an important part in our success with that case. On all of the cases
that Susan became involved with since then, she continued to
impress all of the partners and senior associates with whom she
worked.

I know that Bob Abrams, who served as Susan's mentor for
these many years, will particularly miss her. But Bob also told me

that Susan has learned all he has to teach her, and that it is indeed the time for her to move on to bigger and better things. When Susan was offered an opportunity to come in as a partner at Weiss Weinberg, he encouraged her to take it with his blessing.

And so it is that we will have to say farewell to Susan. Susan, we thank you for all that you have done for us over the years. We thank you for your hard work. We thank you for being a friendly colleague and co-worker, whose warmth and good humor have continually brightened the halls of this office. We will sorely miss you, but we wish you the best of luck in your new position.

Loss, as Emperor Antoninus commented, is really just a form of change, and change can and often does present an opportunity for all involved. While we are saddened to lose Susan, we can also look forward to welcoming new faces, and whatever unique experiences those individuals bring with them. We hope they will prove as smart, resourceful, and enthusiastic as Susan has been.

PAYING TRIBUTE TO AN HONOREE

They say that actions speak more than words. It only follows that if you want to judge a man's character, you look at more than what he says; you look at what he does. Dr. Mark Allen knew that to make a new pediatrics intensive care facility a reality, it would take more than words, so he personally took action. He knew that sitting around complaining about the hospital's lack of resources, or repeatedly making demands of the board of directors would not be enough to bring that new facility to fruition. So, he personally raised the funds to make it happen. Today, we honor Dr. Mark Allen for those tireless efforts. But we also pay tribute to him for much more. We pay tribute to the fine doctor, colleague, and friend he has shown himself to be time and time again, through his words and his actions.

Do you want to know what kind of a person Mark Allen is? I'll tell you a story that will show you what kind of a person he is. When I was a young pediatrics intern at this hospital many years ago, Dr. Allen was the first resident I was assigned to. On my very first day of work, I had a fender-bender on the way to the hospital and, as a result, showed up more than thirty minutes late. Having heard all kinds of nightmarish stories about how the residents could come down on the interns for the slightest of infractions, I came to the hospital prepared to be seriously chewed out. Instead, Dr. Allen, hearing about the accident, expressed genuine concern about how I was. Then he called his mechanic and arranged to have my car picked up and repaired. But he did more than that. At the end of the shift, he drove me home. And he picked me up the next day, and drove me home the next night. He drove me back and forth to work every day until my car was fixed.

Now that I've gotten to know him much better, I realize that his kind treatment of me that day is typical of his interactions with all the doctors, nurses, and patients in this hospital. I learned that day that Dr. Mark Allen is that rare kind of doctor who, in an age when doctors are too often stereotyped as cold, self-involved automatons, genuinely likes working with other people and, without making a big deal of it, without having to be asked, will often go out of his way to do a favor for someone or help them out when they're in need.

You want to know what kind of a doctor Mark Allen is? Ask the nurses who work here. They'll tell you, as they told me when I asked them that question earlier this week, that he's the kind of doctor who not only knows them all by name, but always remembers their birthdays with a card and flowers.

What kind of a doctor is Mark Allen? Ask his patients. They'll tell you he's the kind of doctor who expresses sincere interest in who they are, taking the time to chat about their likes and hobbies, to talk about the latest popular movie or TV show. One patient told me that Dr. Allen, after learning that her favorite author is Charles Dickens, brought her his copy of *Great Expectations* to read while she was recovering from surgery. He's also the kind of doctor, his patients tell me, who always treats them with compassion and dignity, answering their questions and concerns with the utmost consideration and respect.

What kind of doctor is Mark Allen? Ask his colleagues, the other doctors who work in this hospital. They'll tell you he's the kind of doctor they admire, the one who sets a standard for a certain kind of conscientious patient care they strive to match. I know that's certainly been the case with myself. I can say with utmost confidence that I wouldn't be the doctor I am today were it not for his fine example that I have made it my personal goal to emulate.

Talk to his colleagues, the nurses, and his patients, and they'll tell you what kind of doctor Mark Allen is. But if you want to see what kind of person he is, look at his actions and what those actions have achieved—a glorious new facility that is helping save hundreds of children's lives. For achieving that, for being a man of action, we pay tribute today, just as we honor him for being the caring, compassionate, and inspiring figure who we have the great privilege of working with each day.

INTRODUCING A GUEST SPEAKER

I have the great pleasure today of introducing you to someone who, in addition to being my favorite writer, I am fortunate to consider a mentor and a close friend. As it happens, Quentin James was also the first acquaintance I made when I began teaching at Columbia in 1992. I had just been hired as an instructor in the creative writing program, and had been in my new office for about ten minutes, when Quentin walked in. I of course knew who he was; the man, after all, had just won the Pulitzer Prize for *Dogcatcher*. But he introduced himself anyway, and then, to my surprise and my delight, sat in the chair opposite my desk, and proceeded to engage me in conversation. I just couldn't believe that this famous author, who I personally considered one of today's greatest novelists, was taking the time to sit and talk with me. I was even more surprised when he proceeded to inform me, after forty-five minutes chatting together, that I was actually sitting in his office! After I turned bright red and finished sputtering my apology, I asked him why he didn't kick me out when he first came in and found me at his desk. And I'll never forget his response. He smiled and said, "Because I like the company."

In retrospect, I realize that I shouldn't have been quite as surprised by that first meeting as I was. Because anyone who reads Quentin James' novels knows that only someone who has that kind of fascination with other people could create the wonderful, absolutely believable characters that he's famous for. I'm thinking of characters like Evelyn, the alcoholic nightclub singer of *Blue Streak*, and Derek, the cop who dreams of a career as a chef in *Walking the Beat*—characters who are such unique, fully drawn individuals that we feel we know them, and who, when we've reached the last page, we find ourselves missing.

During one of our many conversations about writing, I once asked Quentin about the process he uses to create these characters who are not only realistic but also captivating, complicated individuals. And he told me, "It's easy. I just listen to what people have to say about themselves. Anything you need to know about creating characters you can learn from listening to the people you meet."

As far back as high school, Quentin demonstrated that keen interest in listening to what people have to say. Serving as the editor of his school newspaper, the *Gryphon Gazette*, he wrote a weekly column in which he profiled some student or teacher whom he'd interviewed. That column won him an award from the High School Press Association, and led to a summer internship at the Washington Post. In college, Quentin continued writing these profiles for the Princeton paper. Acting further on his interest in people, and demonstrating the remarkable compassion and empathy that critics today describe as hallmarks of his writing, he also began volunteering his time at a peer crisis counseling center.

The experience of listening to his fellow students share their crises and troubles, and reveal in many cases their most intimate emotions and desires, became the inspiration for Quentin's first novel, *Hear Hear*, published by Random House in 1973 to universal acclaim. Arlene Kreig, reviewing the book in the *New York Times*, hailed it as the arrival of an important new talent in

American fiction. That impressive debut was followed by five more novels and three short story collections, all of which have earned tremendous critical praise and accolades. Four of those novels have been turned into successful films, the most recent one, *The Last Train of the Night* earning Quentin an Oscar for his screenplay. That Oscar can take its place alongside Quentin's Pulitzer, and two American Book awards.

Quentin is currently at work on his next novel, tentatively titled, *For Crying Out Loud.* Today, we have the great privilege of having him here to read an excerpt from it in person, as well as talk to us more about his distinctive writing process. Please, join me in welcoming the wonderful writer responsible for creating all of those marvelous characters who we know and love, my friend, colleague, and occasional office mate, Quentin James.

WELCOME TO CONVENTION/CONFERENCE

I'm here to officially welcome you all to the 32nd annual convention of the American Association of Media Practitioners and Developers. It's entirely appropriate that this year's convention take place over Columbus Day Weekend, when we honor an explorer who bravely set out to explore new worlds. This year's convention, focusing on "Cutting Edge Developments in New Media," offers all of us the opportunity to explore exciting new terrain. I invite all of you to approach this year's events with Columbus's "spirit of discovery" in mind, taking advantage of the many ways in which you too might explore the unfamiliar—and discover a great deal in the process.

First, the various panels that have been organized for the next three days promise exciting revelations for all who attend them. Each panel, which will consist of at least three renowned speakers who are experts in their respective fields, will address a major topic or issue related to New Media, such as "Children's Safety and the Net" and "Synergies: Aligning New Media with Other Entertainment Venues." You might learn more about a topic with which you were already familiar; or you might also find yourself discovering a whole new world of ideas and information you didn't know existed. Either way, you'll have many opportunities to explore fascinating new terrain with these reputable speakers.

Second, the key note address will provide, for all of us, an important window into the world of the future. We are privileged to have as our key note speaker Margaret Anderson, the chair of the Media Studies program at Harvard University and the acclaimed author of the international bestseller *Mediaworld*, who is widely regarded as the world's leading expert in the analysis of the societal effects of media technologies. In her address, titled "Tomorrow and Tomorrow and Tomorrow: The New Media Future," Dr. Anderson will assess the various ways in which current new media technology is shaping the future. That address will take place tomorrow, following lunch, in the Crystal Ballroom.

Third, throughout the conference, you are invited to explore the "New Media Technologies" trade show on the convention floor, where you're likely to make any number of thrilling discoveries. Here, you'll find various demonstrations and samples of the latest Internet products, services, and technologies being developed—including the first "virtual reality" Web site, and an "interactive movie database".

Finally, as you attend these various events, keep in mind that other people can also serve as doorways to new worlds. Hearing of someone else's background and experiences can often make for fascinating discoveries that can educate and profoundly affect us. So take advantage of this rare gathering of hundreds of people working in the same field to meet one another, talk with one another, and learn from one another.

In conclusion, I welcome you once again to our 32nd annual convention: "Cutting Edge Developments in New Media." Now, to quote another great explorer, it's time for you to "boldly go where no man has gone before, to explore strange new worlds." Enjoy the journey.

Index

FIND MORE ON THIS TOPIC BY VISITING
BusinessTown.com
The Web's big site for growing businesses!

☑ **Separate channels on all aspects of starting and running a business**

☑ **Lots of info of how to do business online**

☑ **1,000+ pages of savvy business advice**

☑ **Complete web guide to thousands of useful business sites**

☑ **Free e-mail newsletter**

☑ **Question and answer forums, and more!**

http://www.businesstown.com